Improving the Regulatory Review Process: Industry and Regulatory Initiatives

CMR Workshop Series

Monitoring for Adverse Drug Reactions
Editors: S.R. Walker and A. Goldberg

Long-Term Animal Studies
Their Predictive Value for Man
Editors: S.R. Walker and A.D. Dayan

Medicines and Risk/Benefit Decisions
Editor: S.R. Walker and A.W. Asscher

Quality of Life: Assessment and Application
Editors: S.R. Walker and R.M. Rosser

International Medicines Regulations
A Forward Look to 1992
Editors: S.R. Walker and J.P. Griffin

Animal Toxicity Studies: Their Relevance for Man
Editors: C.E. Lumley and S.R. Walker

Creating the Right Environment for Drug Discovery
Editor: S.R. Walker

Current Issues in Reproductive and Developmental Toxicology
Can an International Guideline be Achieved?
Editors: C.E. Lumley and S.R. Walker

The Carcinogenicity Debate
Editors: J.A.N. McAuslane, C.E. Lumley and S.R. Walker

The Relevance of Ethnic Factors in the Clinical Evaluation of Medicines
Editors: S.R. Walker, C.E. Lumley and J.A.N. McAuslane

Workshop Series

Improving the Regulatory Review Process: Industry and Regulatory Initiatives

Edited by

Cyndy Lumley and Stuart Walker

Centre for Medicines Research
Carshalton, Surrey, UK

Proceedings of a CMR Workshop held at Nutfield Priory,
Nutfield, UK, September 1995

WKAP ARCHIEF

KLUWER ACADEMIC PUBLISHERS
DORDRECHT / BOSTON / LONDON

Distributors

for the United States and Canada: Kluwer Academic Publishers, PO Box 358,
Accord Station, Hingham, MA 02018-0358, USA
for all other countries: Kluwer Academic Publishers Group,
Distribution Center, PO Box 322, 3300 AH Dordrecht, The Netherlands

A catalogue record for this book is available from the British Library

ISBN 0-7923-8706-6

Published in the United Kingdom by Kluwer Academic Publishers,
PO Box 55, Lancaster, UK.

Kluwer Academic Publishers incorporates the publishing programmes of
D. Reidel, Martinus Nijhoff, Dr W. Junk and MTP Press.

Lasertypeset by Martin Lister Publishing Services, Bolton-le-Sands, Carnforth, Lancs.

Printed in Great Britain by Hartnolls Ltd., Bodmin, Cornwall

Contents

Contents

Preface

The Eleventh International Workshop organised by the Centre for Medicines Research was held at Nutfield Priory in Surrey in September 1995. This two-day meeting brought together invited representatives from the pharmaceutical industry and the regulatory agencies in Europe, the United States, Canada, Australia and Japan to discuss industry and regulatory initiatives for improving the regulatory review process.

At a time when the pharmaceutical industry is actively reviewing the drug development process and the majority of companies are examining a variety of ways by which they can achieve a greater efficiency in their development programmes and bring products more rapidly to the marketplace, it was timely that representatives from the industry and the regulatory authorities should meet to look at the current regulatory review process. For many countries, the overall review from market application to approval occupies between one and three years. This can represent up to 25% of overall drug development time which in 1995 was just over 11 years from synthesis to first marketing authorisation for new chemical entities reaching the market.

There is a continuing need for new medicines to reach patients as quickly as possible without, of course, compromising safety. By arranging a workshop of this kind and focusing on those factors which contribute to the time spent on regulatory review, an important component of drug development time, it was possible to identify areas in which there could be room for improvement.

The workshop got off to a lively start by David Jefferys (MCA) presenting his personal view on what determines the speed of review, namely, the need for the product, quality of the dossier or the efficiency of the regulatory authorities. This was followed by three companies – a biotechnology company, a Japanese company and a major international company – describing their strategies to ensure a quick and efficient review.

The second session allowed a number of leading regulators to describe various initiatives to improve the review process. This included a discussion of conditional licensing, the importance of dialogue and interaction between regulators and sponsors, the use of electronic dossiers or CANDAs, the exchange of assessment reports and the training of assessors, the regulatory assessment report in the new European system, as well as the use of industry expert reports, internal and external experts and advisory boards by the regulatory authorities.

With this background, part of the second day was devoted to syndicate groups who spent the morning brainstorming and preparing for a feedback session where recommendations to the industry as well as to the regulatory authorities to improve the review process were presented. Finally, there was a discussion of the strategies that should be considered for implementation by the end of the Century. This included an industry perspective as well as a commentary from the MHW in Japan, the EMEA and the FDA.

This was one of the most lively and interactive workshops that the CMR has held. It provided a very stimulating environment for a most productive debate and the standard of presentation was extremely high. The meeting was ably chaired by Fernand Sauer, Executive Director of the EMEA, Kathryn Zoon, Director of the Center for Biologics Evaluation and Research (FDA) and Peter Read, Chairman of Hoechst Marion Roussel UK.

It is important that following such a workshop, the proceedings should be made available to a wider audience in the hope of stimulating further debate and discussion on this important topic. The editors would like to thank all the authors and participants for their contribution to this meeting and Brenda Mullinger who has provided so much editorial support for these proceedings. In particular, we are indebted to Sandra Cox, whose work as administrator and compiler has made a major contribution to the quality and timeliness of this publication.

It is hoped that some of the ideas explored during this meeting will form the basis of future workshops organised by the Centre for Medicines Research.

Cyndy Lumley
Stuart Walker
March 1996

Foreword

The new system for the free movement of medicinal products within the European Union became operational in February 1995, with the new European Medicines Evaluation Agency (EMEA) seated in London. In essence, these new measures are intended to promote the free circulation of medicinal products within the European Union, while reinforcing the protection of public health. In particular, they permit the rapid access of new products to a continental scale market. A single evaluation of the highest possible scientific quality can be undertaken through the new European Medicines Evaluation Agency, working in close partnership with the Member States and the European Commission.

I therefore particularly welcomed the initiative taken by the Centre for Medicines Research to organise a workshop to deal with the necessary improvements to the regulatory review process. I was particularly pleased to note the participation of colleagues from prestigious national drug agencies in the European Union, the United States, Japan, Canada and Australia, as well as eminent regulatory affairs specialists from the pharmaceutical industry. Within the context of current activities of the ICH process (International Conference on Harmonisation of Technical Requirements for Registration of Pharmaceuticals for Human Use) between the EU, Japan and the USA, the EMEA has already made an important technical contribution. Exchanging views and ideas with our national and international partners is particularly useful for the EMEA during this initial phase of setting up new structures and practices.

The new-look Committee for Proprietary Medicinal Products (CPMP) and Committee for Veterinary Medicinal Products (CVMP) have become fully functioning independent scientific committees. With this new organisation, they have also each created a number of permanent and *ad hoc* working groups. The new scientific emphasis of the committees' work has been strengthened by their access to over 1,600 experts on the Agency's European experts list.

Six months from its inauguration on 26th January 1995, the EMEA and the new European centralised drug registration system have started working rather satisfactorily, in particular the so-called "centralised procedure", leading to a single marketing authorisation, valid throughout the European Union. Better information for health professionals and consumers through harmonised Summary of Product Characteristics (SmPCs) and package leaflets is a central part of the EMEA's work. As part of this commitment, the Agency makes the scientific assessment report (European Public Assessment Reports – EPARs) available to the public once the Commission decision is taken.

Another innovation is that companies can now ask the EMEA, through its committees, for scientific advice long before they make an application, and several requests have been received, which are currently being examined. The EMEA is also responsible for the co-ordination of national activities in respect of post-marketing surveillance (pharmacovigilance), inspection and laboratory controls, to ensure the safety of medicinal products circulating within the Community.

The support and commitment of all national authorities and of the European Commission in terms of time and resources has been a vital element in the functioning of the Agency. This solid support has allowed for the smooth development of an Agency and a regulatory review process in which industry can have confidence. Scientific quality, but also review time, will be the key performance indicators to judge the merits of the new regulatory process emerging in Europe and to benchmark it against its prestigious counterparts in the world.

Fernand Sauer
Executive Director, EMEA
March 1996

Notes on Contributors and Chairmen

Professor Rolf Bass MD is Head of Unit for Human Medicines at the European Agency for the Evaluation of Medicinal Products (EMEA) a post he has held since April 1995. From 1979 until 1995 he was Head of Drug Toxicology and Director and professor at the Federal Institute for Drugs and Medical Devices in Berlin. From 1984 until 1991 he was Chairman of the Safety Working Party of the Committee for Proprietary Medicinal Products (CPMP) of the European Communities. He has published over 150 papers in the areas of mitochondriogenesis, pre- and postnatal toxicology, transplacental pharmacokinetics, toxicological requirements for safety assessment of drugs for registration, safety requirements for biotechnology products, animal experimentation, formaldehyde, risk assessment and risk management.

André Broekmans MD PhD is Executive Director of the Medicines Evaluation Board, in the Netherlands. Prior to becoming the Executive Director, he held the post of Head of Department of Clinical Assessment of the Medicines Evaluation Board and between 1987–1990 was Head of Medical Affairs at the Netherlands Heart Foundation. Dr Broekmans is a member of the Pharmaceutical Committee of the European Commission and a member of the Management Board of the European Medicines Evaluation Agency. He is currently Chairman of the Pharmaceutical Evaluation Report Scheme.

Emily Donnelly BSc(Pharm) MPSI MRPharmS is Director and Senior Vice President, Transnational Regulatory Affairs and Compliance at SmithKline Beecham Pharmaceuticals. She has responsibility worldwide for all regulatory activities and compliance and is a member of many SmithKline Beecham Pharmaceuticals' Management Committees. Emily was actively involved in the merger of SmithKline Beckman and Beecham Pharmaceuticals. She has worked in the pharmaceutical industry for 25 years and is a member of both the Pharmaceutical Society of Ireland and the Royal Pharmaceutical Society of Great Britain. As a pharmacist, Emily's experience includes – working in quality control, manufacturing, formulation development and as a medical representative. She has also worked in wholesale pharmacy, retail and hospital pharmacy. She spent five years with The Association of the British Pharmaceutical Industry (ABPI) working on scientific, medical and regulatory activities and has worked for Leo Pharmaceuticals and Merrell Dow Pharmaceuticals.

Professor Alfred G Hildebrandt MD is Head of the German Federal Institute for Drugs and Medical Devices, Berlin. After spending several years at the Universities of Pennsylvania and Texas, he held the post of senior resident in the Clinical Pharmacology Department and later Professor of Pharmacology and Toxicology at the Free University, Berlin. He then became Dean and Medical Director of the University Hospital, Klinikum Steglitz, also at the Free University, Berlin. Before taking up his current post, he was the Head of the Max von Pettenkofer Institute of the German Federal Health Office (responsible for evaluation of risks to the health of consumers from foods and chemicals). He is also a member of the Committee for Proprietary Medicinal Products and Chairman of the CPMP's Efficacy working party.

Maria Holz-Slomczyk MD, a specialist in internal medicine and gastroenterology, is Head of the Review Department of the German Federal Institute for Drugs and Medical Devices, Berlin. In this function she is in charge of the medical review of "old drugs" on the market. Previously, she was responsible for the approval and registration of drugs in the field of gastroenterology and metabolism, and later was the Head of the Division of Cardiovascular Drugs. Her specialities include drug information for professionals and patients as well as bioavailability and bioequivalence issues.

David B Jefferys BSc MD FRCP FRCP(Ed) FFPM is Director, Licensing Division, at the Medicines Control Agency, UK. He is a physician by training and held various posts in clinical and academic medicine before joining the Department of Health in 1984. He worked on the review of medicines and in pharmacovigilance before becoming the Principal Medical Officer in charge of new drug licensing in 1986 and became Business Manager in charge of new drugs and European licensing in 1989 with the creation of the Medicines Control Agency. He is a past Chairman of the Pharmaceutical Evaluation Report Scheme. He is one of the UK members of the CPMP and was the Chairman of the Operational Working Party of the former CPMP. Dr Jefferys is Visiting Professor in Medicine at the University of Newcastle.

Gorm Jensen MD DMSc is Chairman of the Danish Board of Registration and is one of the Danish members of the CPMP. He is a clinician with specialist degrees in Cardiology and Internal Medicine, and is Chief Physician, Department of Cardiology, Hvidovre Hospital, and associate Professor of Cardiology, University of Copenhagen. He has published more than 120 papers on various topics, focusing on cardiovascular epidemiology and clinical trials in cardiovascular medicine. He has worked as medical assessor and expert for the Danish Medical Agency since the late 1970s.

Cyndy Lumley BSc PhD is Associate Director at the Centre for Medicines Research (CMR). Her current research interests include pharmaceutical R&D expenditure and strategies, efficiency in international drug development, the regulatory review process and the rationalisation of carcinogenicity test design. Prior to joining CMR, she obtained degrees in Medical Biochemistry (University of Surrey) and Radiation Biology (University of London). She is currently Chairman of the British Toxicology Society Executive Committee, a member of the American College of Toxicology, sits on the Editorial Board of TEN and is an active contributor to scientific publications and meetings.

Neil McAuslane BSc MSc PhD is Research Manager at the Centre for Medicines Research, with responsibility for managing the innovation, safety evaluation and regulations programme. He joined the Centre in 1988 as a Postdoctoral Fellow in affiliation with the Division of Clinical Pharmacy, University of Wales, Cardiff, and became a permanent member of staff in 1991. Dr McAuslane received his PhD degree in Clinical Pharmacology from the University of Edinburgh, having gained an MSc in Toxicology at the University of Surrey and a BSc in Pharmacology from Dundee University. His current areas of research include an evaluation of regulatory review times of pharmaceuticals and the innovative output of the pharmaceutical industry. He has edited four books and co-authored several of the Centre's publications and reports.

Dann M Michols MBA BComm(Hons) is Director General of the Canadian Drugs Directorate. In January, 1993, Mr Michols assumed responsibility for the management of Canada's drug regulation agency to implement the recommendations of the Gagnon Report and other similar exercises leading to a renewed Drugs Directorate. He also has responsibilities within Health Canada to facilitate initiatives in the area of national pharmaceutical policy and regulation and to co-ordinate the results into a comprehensive and cohesive pharmaceutical policy for Canada. Prior to this assignment, Mr Michols was Director of Operations for the federal Royal Commission on New Reproductive Technologies, responsible for the development and management of all consultation, communication, co-ordination, and policy analysis activities. Mr Michols has had a 25-year career in the Canadian Public Service, the last 12 years of which at the level of Assistant Deputy Minister.

Kaoru Misawa BSc MSc graduated from the Department of Pharmaceutical Sciences, the University of Tokyo in 1984 and took a Masters Degree in Biochemistry at the same university. He joined the Ministry of Health and Welfare (MHW) in 1986 and started his career in the field of ADR information. He was seconded by the Japanese government to the World Health Organization where he spent two years working for the pharmaceutical unit. Since 1993 he has been the International Conference on Harmonisation co-ordinator for the MHW.

Abraham P Morgenstern PhD graduated in organic chemistry/pharmaco-chemistry in 1965 at the Free University of Amsterdam and obtained his PhD in 1969. He worked for two years on projects concerning structure–activity relationships of new molecules in the Research and Development Division of the Dutch chemical pharmaceutical company Gist-brocades. Since 1972 he held positions in Regulatory Affairs in Gist-brocades. He is now Director, Corporate Regulatory Affairs of Yamanouchi Europe BV (the former pharmaceutical Division of Gist-brocades which was acquired by Yamanouchi Pharmaceutical Company Limited, Tokyo, in 1991). He is member of the ad hoc expert group: "Regulatory Affairs" of the European Federation of Pharmaceutical Industries' Associations (EFPIA). He has lectured on various occasions and published on subjects related to regulatory affairs.

Peter R Read MB BS DSc(Hon) FFPM qualified in medicine at Charing Cross Hospital Medical School, University of London in 1964. Following various clinical appointments, he joined the pharmaceutical division of Hoechst in 1971 and was appointed to the Board of Hoechst UK in 1987 with responsibility for life sciences. Dr Read is currently Chairman of Hoechst UK Limited and Hoechst Marion Roussel UK. He is also Chairman of A H Cox and Company Limited, Behring Diagnostics UK Limited, and a Board Member of Hoechst Schering AgrEvo UK Limited. Dr Read has been actively involved in The Association of the British Pharmaceutical Industry over many years and is now President-elect. He also chaired the Centre for Medicines Research Policy Board between 1989 and 1993.

Fernand Sauer is the Executive Director of the newly created European Agency for the Evaluation of Medicinal Products (EMEA) in London. He is a qualified pharmacist from the University of Strasbourg. He subsequently received a Masters in European and International Law from the University of Paris and various post-graduate diplomas in public health, pharmaceutical legislation and European Community Studies. From 1972 to 1979 Mr Sauer held various positions in France as hospital pharmacist and pharmaceutical inspector at the Ministry of Health. In 1979 he joined the European Commission in Brussels (DG III) as Administrator and in 1985 he became Head of Pharmaceuticals. He has been involved in the completion of the European Internal Market, trilateral harmonisation of regulatory requirements (ICH) between the EC, the USA and Japan and the development of pricing transparency and industrial policy in the pharmaceutical sector.

David R Savello BPharm MSc PhD is Vice President of North American Regulatory Affairs for Glaxo Wellcome Inc. He joined Glaxo in 1985 as Director of Pharmaceutical Development and was Vice President of Development for several years prior to 1992. Before joining Glaxo, Dr Savello worked for Warner-Lambert in the area of pharmaceutics research and development. Previously, he was employed by Boehringer Ingelheim Limited in Connecticut, where he established and managed that company's US Pharmaceutics R&D Department before moving to Germany to become their International Director of Pharmaceutics R&D. He also worked for Riker Laboratories in St Pauls, Minnesota, where he was head of the Pharmaceutics R&D Department. Additionally he was an adjunct Professor at the University of Minnesota School of Pharmacy from 1975–1978. Dr Savello serves on the University of North Carolina School of Pharmacy Board of Visitors, the North Carolina State University School of Physical and Mathematical Science Foundation Board, and the University of Kentucky College of Pharmacy Advisory Council. He is also a member of the American Association of Pharmaceutical Scientists, the American Association for the Advancement of Science, and the Drug Information Association.

Eve E Slater MD is the Senior Vice President, Clinical and Regulatory Development, Merck Research Laboratories, USA. Her responsibilities include supervision of Merck's late phase development programmes and research on the medical and health outcomes of therapy with Merck's medicines. She also serves as scientific liaison for Johnson & Johnson Merck Consumer Health Group and is responsible for Research Public Affairs. Prior to joining Merck, she held an academic appointment at Harvard Medical School, Boston, where she was Chief of the Hypertension Unit of the Massachusetts General Hospital. Dr Slater is currently Adjunct Associate Clinical Professor of Medicine at Columbia University's College of Physicians and Surgeons. Her major current research interest is the assessment of disease risk factors. She formerly contributed to the biochemistry of the renin–angiotensin system, hypertension/aortic diseases, mechanisms of insulin resistance and adrenergic receptor systems. Dr Slater has served as a member of the Publications Committee of the Council for High Blood Pressure Research, American Heart Association, and is a fellow of the American College of Internal Medicine and the American College of Cardiology. She is also a representative of the US Pharmaceutical Research and Manufacturers Association and is chair of the International Conference on Harmonisation's Efficacy Task Force: Committee on the Structure and Content of Clinical Study Reports.

Ralph Smalling BSc MSc is Director, Regulatory Affairs at Amgen Inc. Mr Smalling has worked at Amgen in both scientific and regulatory capacities, and he was integrally involved in the scientific development and regulatory licensure of Epoetin alfa and in the licensure of Filgrastim. He is currently responsible for the management of all aspects of Regulatory Affairs activities for Amgen US and certain Amgen international offices. Mr Smalling has served as faculty member and as course director for both US and international regulatory seminars. He served as a member of the pharmaceutical subcommittee of the US/Japan Bilateral Forum in Biotechnology, sponsored by the US – Japan Business Council, and more recently as a member of the BIO FDA Reform Task Group. Mr Smalling received his Bachelor's degree in Biology from Occidental College (1977) and Master's degree in Microbiology from California State University (1981).

Professor Kjell Strandberg PhD MD is Director General of Medical Products Agency, Sweden, a post he has held since July 1990. He has been a lecturer in Clinical Pharmacology and Pulmonary Medicine, Head of the Pharmacotherapeutic Division, and Director of the Department of Drugs, National Board of Health and Welfare, as well as Head of the Division of Clinical Pharmacology, University

Hospital in Uppsala, Sweden. He is a member of the Nordic Council of Medicine, the Royal Swedish Academy of Engineering Sciences, the EU Pharmaceutical Committee and the EU Committee for Proprietary Medicinal Products (CPMP). He has published papers in allergology, pharmacology, clinical pharmacology and drug control.

Robert Temple MD is Associate Director for Medical Policy in the Food and Drug Administration's (FDA) Center for Drug Evaluation and Research. He also heads one of the Center's five Offices of Drug Evaluation, the offices that are responsible for review of marketing applications. He has worked at the FDA since 1972 and has been a primary reviewer of applications as well as Director of the Division of Cardio-Renal Drug Products. He is particularly interested in, and has published on, the design and analysis of clinical trials intended to show equivalence of two products, trials intended to show dose–response relationships, the ethics of placebo controls and of controlled trials generally in serious illness, study designs utilising "enrichment" approaches to make success more probable, and evaluation of subsets of the overall study population.

Professor Stuart R Walker BSc PhD(Lond) CChem CBiol FRSC FIBiol FInstD FRCPath is the Director of the Centre for Medicines Research in the UK and Honorary Professor of Pharmaceutical Medicine, University of Wales, Cardiff. He spent ten years at London University which included lectureships in biochemical pharmacology at St Mary's Hospital Medical School and in clinical pharmacology at the Cardiothoracic Institute in London. This was followed by eight years with Glaxo Group Research in the UK where he had international responsibility for several of their clinical research programmes. His current research interests include studies into the process of innovation in drug research and development, an examination of the impact of international medicines regulations and policy issues on drug development, investigating the role as well as the predictive value of preclinical animal toxicology and measuring the socioeconomic benefit of medicines including quality of life in therapeutic intervention studies. Professor Walker is a member of several academic, professional and industrial committees and sits on the editorial boards of three scientific journals. He is frequently involved in the organisation of national and international meetings on key issues that concern the pharmaceutical industry and has lectured extensively throughout Europe, Japan and the USA. Professor Walker has co-authored over 150 research papers and edited 15 books.

Roger L Williams MD is the Deputy Center Director for Pharmaceutical Science, Center for Drug Evaluation and Research, Food and Drug Administration (FDA). He was appointed to this position in October of 1995 and in this capacity, directs a new Office of Pharmaceutical Sciences in the Center, with oversight responsibility for the Office of New Drug Chemistry, the Office of Generic Drugs, the Office of Clinical Pharmacology and Biopharmaceutics, the Office of Research and Testing, and other Center functions. He has responsibility for the Center's international activities and is the FDA's lead representative to the International Conference on Harmonisation. Dr Williams' career in the FDA began in 1990 when he accepted the position of Director, Office of Generic Drugs, in the Center for Drug Evaluation and Research. In August of 1993, Dr Williams became Associate Director for Science and Medical Affairs in the Center. Prior to joining the FDA, Dr Williams conducted over 400 separate clinical investigations on drug safety and efficacy and drug product quality and testing. He has authored over 100 publications and is board certified in internal medicine and in clinical pharmacology.

Kathryn C Zoon PhD became Director of the Center for Biologics Evaluation Research (CBER), Food and Drug Administration, in March 1992. Dr Zoon was formerly the Director of the Division of Cytokine Biology in CBER, where she was actively involved with regulatory issues related to cytokines, growth factors and studies on interferon purification, characterisation and interferon receptors. Dr Zoon worked at NIH from 1975 to 1980, with Nobel Prize Laureate Christian B Anfinsen on the production and purification of human interferons. She received her BS degree, *cum laude*, in chemistry from Rensselaer Polytechnic Institute in 1970 and was granted a PhD in biochemistry from The Johns Hopkins University in 1976. Dr Zoon is an editor of the Journal of Interferon Research and the author of numerous scientific papers on interferons. She has received numerous awards, including the NIH Lectureship 1994, Sydney Riegelman Lectureship 1994, Biopharm Person of the Year Award 1992, Genetic Engineering News (GEN) Award 1994 for streamlining and improving the regulatory process for biologics and biotechnology products, and the Meritorious Executive Rank Award 1994 for sustained superior performance in revitalising and reorganising the Center for Biologics Evaluation and Research to meet the challenges of new responsibilities and new technologies.

1 International regulatory review times

NEIL McAUSLANE and STUART WALKER

Summary

1. At a time when both companies and regulatory authorities are evaluating their strategies to increase efficiency, it is important to have comparative data on overall development times. Therefore, as the period a new therapeutic candidate spends in regulatory review contributes to the overall development time, it is of value to have information on review times within different authorities.

2. A study has been initiated to collect data on application and approval dates in nine of the major pharmaceutical markets (the USA, Canada, Japan, Australia, the UK, France, Germany, Italy and Spain). Preliminary analyses show differences in review times between authorities, even for the same compounds submitted within a similar time frame.

3. The reasons for differences in review times should be questioned, as all authorities have the same basic tenets, to protect and promote the public health and to review dossiers based on quality, safety and efficacy. In order to understand the reasons behind these differences, other factors need to be assessed, such as the quality of dossiers, companies' response time to authorities' questions and the ability of authorities to manage the review effectively and efficiently.

Introduction

Regulatory review is the last major development hurdle that must be passed by a new chemical entity (NCE) before it reaches the market. This occurs at the end of a lengthy research and development process, which takes on average 9.5 years from synthesis to first application for a product licence. The total development time to launch in the first market will also include the review process which, in the early 1990s, was between 1 and 3 years for the major markets (MacInnes *et al.*, 1995).

Pharmaceutical companies realise that it is necessary to reduce the long development times, both to the first market and to the international market, in order to remain competitive in the future. Although regulatory review is the one step in the process that is not within industry control, companies can influence the duration by submitting a good quality scientific dossier and responding in a timely manner to any questions raised by the reviewer.

Over the last 5 years the regulatory arena has seen a number of changes which have the potential to have a major impact on both review times and the relationship between industry and regulatory authorities (Table 1.1). This has lead to optimism regarding the possibility of improving the review process. At a time when both pharmaceutical companies and regulatory authorities are evaluating their strategies in order to increase efficiency, there is a need for data on review times within different authorities. However, with the exception of a few authorities that publish annual statistics, accurate information is not available. Furthermore, it is difficult to draw

Table 1.1 Factors which may impact on review times in the future

- Harmonisation of technical requirements
- Increase in dialogue between industry and authorities
- New European procedures
- Restructuring and reorganisation of authorities
- Introduction by authorities of fees and target review times

comparisons between authorities based on published data, as different definitions are used with regard to what is included in the review time.

The measurement of total regulatory review times (i.e. time from date of application to date of approval, including any company down time) is one gross way of evaluating the time compounds spend in the review process. A study has therefore been initiated to obtain this information for the major authorities. The objectives are to:

- Obtain data on regulatory review times from 1990 to 1995 in the USA, Canada, Japan, Australia, the UK, France, Germany, Italy and Spain;

- Investigate trends in review times over the last decade;

- Provide data to establish a baseline with which to evaluate authorities and changes that may occur in the future.

Methodology

New chemical entities marketed in the countries of interest between 1990 and 1995 have been identified using the CMR international marketed medicines database (MacInnes *et al.*, 1994). An NCE is defined as any new active substance which has not been available previously for therapeutic use in man and is to be made available as a "Prescription Only Medicine" for the cure, alleviation, prevention or *in vivo* diagnosis of diseases in man. New salts, prodrugs, esters of existing compounds, combination products (unless one of the active constituents has never been marketed previously), vaccines, antigens and veterinary medicines are not included. To date, 46 companies responsible for marketing 275 NCEs between 1990 and 1995 have been asked to provide application and approval dates in the countries of interest, for marketed NCEs and any others which have been approved but not yet marketed. The regulatory authorities in Japan, France, Australia, Canada and Germany have also been asked to identify all approvals during the 1990s and to provide application and approval dates, where possible.

3

To date, 32 pharmaceutical companies in Japan, the USA and Europe have provided data on 213 compounds. Information has also been received from the authorities in Canada, Germany and Australia, and application and approval dates in the USA have been obtained from the public domain (PMA, 1990, 1991, 1992, 1993; PhRMA, 1994). Missing information on compounds known to have been approved in the 1990s is being pursued.

This paper presents preliminary analyses, as full data are not yet available for every country. An indication of the completeness of each data set for each year of approval is provided with the analyses, based on:

$$\frac{\text{Number of compounds with full data}}{\underset{\substack{\text{Number of compounds} \\ \text{known to have been} \\ \text{approved in that year}}}{} + \underset{\substack{\text{Compounds known to have} \\ \text{been marketed in that year, but} \\ \text{for which approval dates are} \\ \text{not known}}}{}} \times 100$$

Trends in total regulatory review times over the last decade

The mean total review times are shown as 3-year moving averages for the USA, Japan, Germany, France, the UK (Figure 1.1), Canada, Australia, Spain and Italy (Figure 1.2). Although still incomplete, these data suggest that compounds may have spent, on average, between 0.75 years (France) and 3.75 years (Spain) in the review process, over the last decade. However, it appears that average review times in five of the major markets are converging on 2 years in the 1990s (Figure 1.1), with the UK and France being the fastest authorities. Improvements have also been seen in the remaining countries, but review times remain at 2.5 years or greater in these markets (Figure 1.2).

4

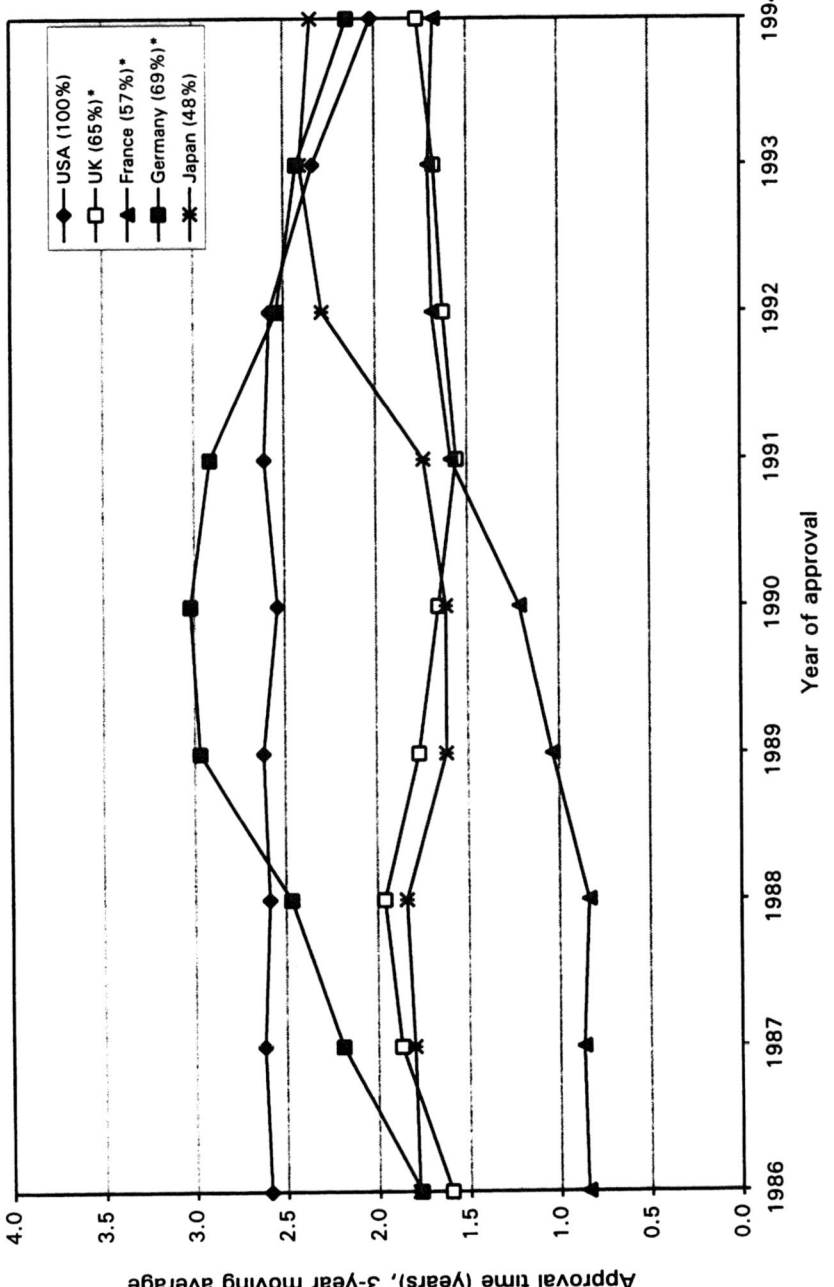

Figure 1.1 Mean regulatory approval times in five countries (1985–1995). Preliminary data

*NB: Three authorisations through the European centralised procedure in 1995 have been excluded. ( ) = % of data available

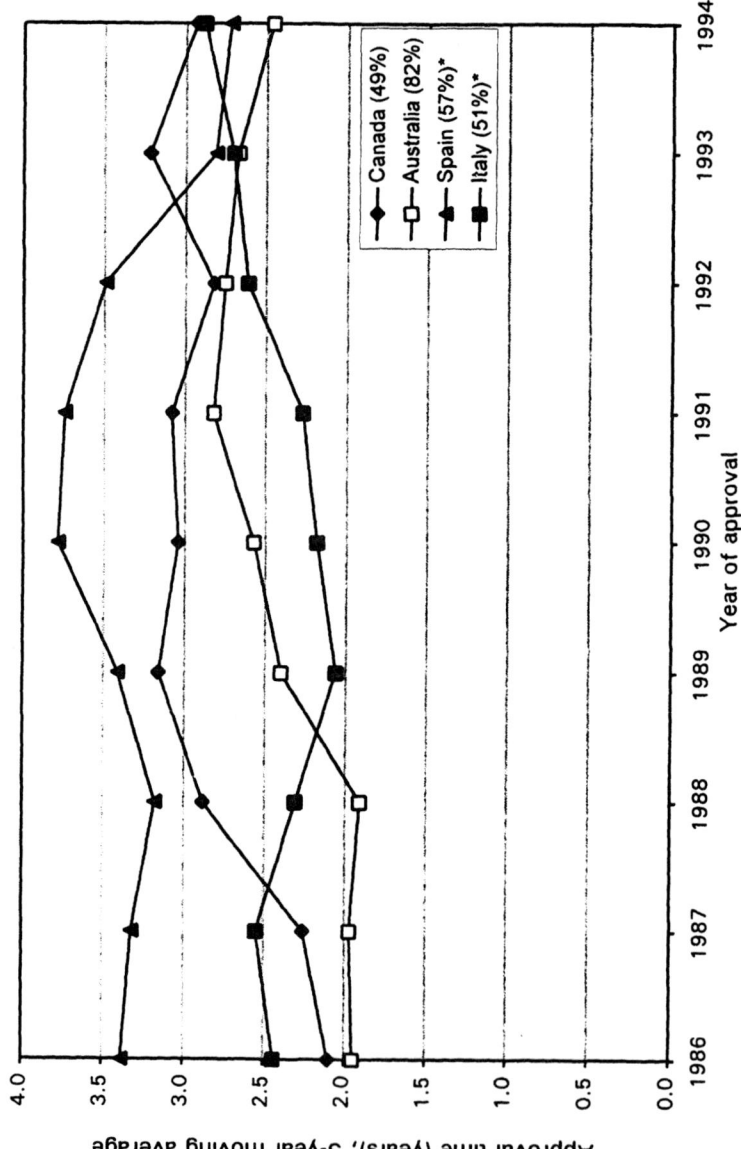

Figure 1.2 Mean regulatory approval times in four countries (1985–1995). Preliminary data

*NB: Three authorisations through the European centralised procedure in 1995 have been excluded. ( ) = % of data available

Total regulatory review times in the 1990s

Although the mean provides the average for all approvals, it can be influenced upwards or downwards by outliers. The median may therefore be more representative of the actual time compounds are spending in the approval process. Data for median review times in the 1990s show a decrease over time in the USA, Germany, Australia and Spain, and an increase in the UK, France, Japan and Italy (Figure 1.3). In 1994–95, median review times were very similar – between 1.3 and 1.5 years – in France, Spain, the UK, the USA and Germany.

Comparison of the UK and the USA

There are limitations to the conclusions that can be drawn from mean or median approval times, particularly as the same compounds were not necessarily submitted or reviewed at the same time in each country. True comparisons can be drawn between authorities only by assessing a cohort of compounds submitted within a similar time frame.

The examination of a group of compounds submitted to both the UK and the USA, within a 6-month period, still shows considerable differences between the total review times (Figure 1.4). Within the latter half of the 1980s, the UK was consistently quicker than the USA at reviewing the same compounds. Over this period, the USA took longer than the UK to review 17/23 of the compounds in this cohort, with the difference being more than 1 year for 11 compounds. In contrast, the UK took longer to review six compounds. The situation has changed in the 1990s, with 6/19 compounds submitted to both authorities being reviewed in virtually the same time. Although the USA took longer than the UK to review nine compounds in the 1990s, the difference was more than 1 year for only two of these.

Discussion

This preliminary analysis of total review times in nine major markets shows that companies can expect their compounds to spend on average between 1.5 and 3 years in the review process, depending

7

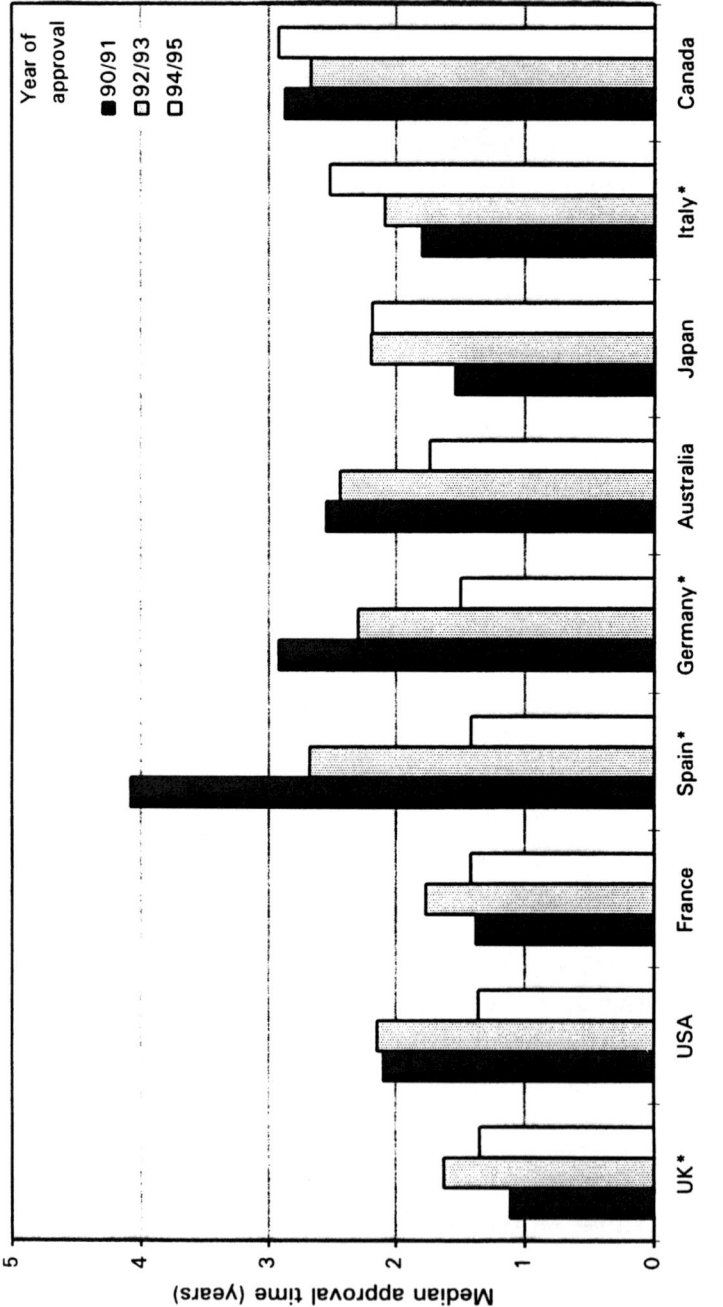

*These exclude three compounds given authorisation through the European centralised procedure in 1995

Figure 1.3 Median regulatory approval times 1990–1995. Preliminary data

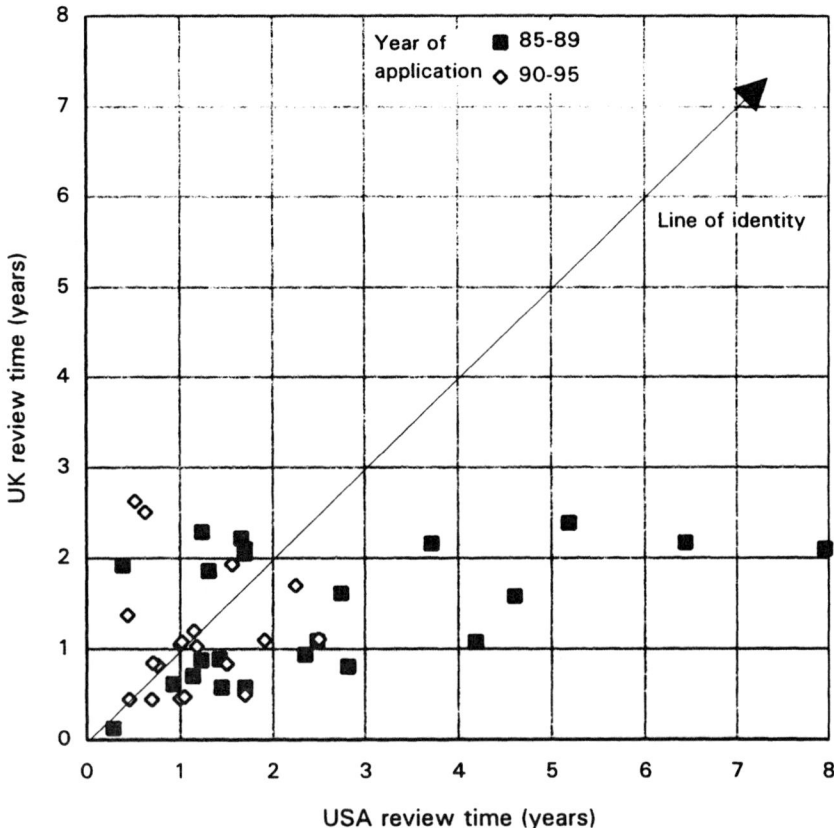

Figure 1.4 Comparison of review times for compounds submitted to the USA and the UK within 6 months

on the authority. Although considerable differences have existed between authorities in the past, it appears that review times are converging at around 2 years in at least five countries – the USA, the UK, Japan, France and Germany. Similar review times in European countries may be partially explained by the use of the concertation or multistate procedures. Indeed, in the future, the approval times for all authorities in Europe should be even more uniform as the new European licensing procedures, which have defined timelines (EC, 1994), are used. The idea of defining the timelines for the assessment of NCEs is becoming more widespread amongst the major regulatory authorities, as user fees are introduced, with the USA, Canada and Australia also having target review times for the assessment of NCEs.

Care must be taken when drawing conclusions based on average total review times, as the same compounds are not being compared across countries. This should become less of a problem in the future, as pharmaceutical companies aim to submit a marketing application in all major markets simultaneously (Donnelly, Ritchie and French, 1996). Thus, in future it may become increasingly difficult to justify differences in review times between agencies, as they will be assessing the same dossier at the same time.

It is apparent that review times vary for the same compounds, even when they are submitted to different authorities within a similar time frame. The reasons for this could be questioned, as all authorities have the same basic tenets, to protect and promote the public health and to review dossiers in terms of quality, safety and efficacy. This suggests that differences in review times between the competent authorities may be related to the way in which the review is managed. Certainly, the approaches vary; for example, more reliance is placed on industry opinion, summaries and expert reports in Europe than in the USA (Barrowcliffe, 1994).

Conclusion

There are differences between the major authorities in total regulatory review times in the 1990s. In order to understand the reasons behind these differences other factors need to be assessed, such as the quality of the dossiers, companies' response time to authorities' questions and the ability of authorities to manage the review effectively and efficiently. Future CMR studies will address these issues.

References

Barrowcliffe S (1994). Developing a global regulatory strategy. *Drug Information Journal*, **28**: 525–531.

Commission of the European Communities: (1994). Draft notice to applicants for marketing authorisation for medicinal products for human use in the European Community. Brussels. 111/5944/94.

Donnelly E, Ritchie, J and French, S (1996). Company strategies to ensure a quick and efficient review: A transnational company. In Lumley CE and Walker SR (eds) *Improving the Regulatory Review Process: Industry and Regulatory Initiatives*, Kluwer Academic Publishers, Lancaster, pp. 41–52.

MacInnes R., Lumley CE and Walker SR (1994). New chemical entity output of the international pharmaceutical industry from 1970 to 1992. *Clinical Pharmacology and Therapeutics*, **56** (3), 339–349.

MacInnes R, MacFarlane FG, Drasdo AL and Lumley CE (1995). International drug development: Efficiency and output (1980–1994). CMR Report – CMR95-54R.

Pharmaceutical Manufacturers Association (1990, 1991, 1992, 1993). New drug approvals.

Pharmaceutical Research and Manufacturers Association (1994). New drug approvals.

2 What determines the speed of review: Need for the product, quality of the dossier or efficiency of regulatory authorities?

DAVID JEFFERYS

Summary

1. Most regulatory authorities have a procedure for accelerated review; the fast-track procedure in the UK is based solely on potential gain for the public health. Industry does not appear to gain time from use of this procedure, from conditional licensing or from authorisation under exceptional circumstances. Hence, need for the product does not seem to be a determinant of speed of review.

2. The regulatory review process worldwide is speeding up; in the UK the average assessment time for new active substances has fallen from 112 days in 1989/90 to 55 days in 1994/95. Such improvements have introduced the requirement for quality assurance in the regulatory process.

3. Initiatives such as increased dialogue, production of early guidelines and training of regulators have all increased efficiency. Electronic dossiers, while providing major benefits to industry and agencies alike, do not appear to speed up the assessment process.

4. The quality of dossiers is variable. Industry must recognise the need to provide an integrated, and not compartmentalised, resource document which provides a critical analysis of data. The summary is particularly important from a European perspective. Worldwide development also needs a regulatory strategy specific for the product and the corporation.

5. To further reduce the overall time to market will require, among other things, close co-operation and partnership between regulators and the industry to improve the quality of regulatory submissions and of the regulatory process.

Introduction

Ten years ago drug regulators saw their role as the narrow one of safeguarding the public health through the efficient and effective assessment of new medicines. The difference today is the recognition that the public health is served not only by the thorough assessment of new medicines but equally by ensuring that new medicines are brought to the patient as rapidly as possible. This significant change is reflected in the mission statements emerging from regulatory authorities across the world.

Drug regulation is also now seen as a partnership between the regulators and the pharmaceutical industry. Each has a clearly defined role and responsibility. It is important that those roles and responsibilities are recognised and respected. However, in a mature relationship it is also important that there is close co-operation and collaboration between the two partners. Some of the ways in which the regulators and the regulated might work together in the interests of patients are discussed in the ensuing papers.

In any such discussion there is danger in focusing solely on new chemical entities (NCEs) or new active substances (NASs). Drug regulation is much wider than that. In the context of the assessment process, industry is just as interested in assessment times for line extensions, abridged applications and variations. From the public health perspective it is also vital to have an efficient and effective pharmacovigilance system and a product surveillance scheme.

As regulators, therefore, we must consider the overall procedure for drug regulation rather than concentrate on one aspect of it. At the Medicines Control Agency (MCA) we are committed to the provision of a rapid, high quality service in all aspects of drug regulation, not simply the assessment of new drug applications.

This paper addresses the three parameters which may influence the speed of review, namely the need for the product, the quality of the dossier and the efficiency of the regulatory process.

Need for the product

To what extent is the need for the product a determinant of the speed of review? There are two elements to consider. The first is the procedures which most regulatory agencies worldwide have for assessing certain applications out of order, such as accelerated review, fast-track procedure and priority assessments. The second issue is facilities for accelerating the development of certain products for licensing under exceptional circumstances.

In the UK the fast-track procedure means that under certain very specialised circumstances the MCA will assess a dossier ahead of turn. The criteria are solely those of a significant potential gain for the public health. In reality such fast-track procedures are only necessary in a time of backlog and delay. At the present time, assessments are completed in under 50 working days so there is very little gain to be had by granting such fast-track status.

Interestingly, only nine applications have sought fast-track status in the UK since its introduction 4 years ago; only two were approved on initial application. The implication is that perhaps the applications were premature. In an earlier study (Rawlins and Jefferys, 1991) on the fate of NAS applications in the UK between 1987 and 1989, there was a significant difference in the first time approval rate for Type IA innovative drugs (Lund Dukes classification, 1980) compared to the Type IIA semi-innovative drugs. There may be a variety of reasons for this, including the risk-to-benefit ratio being more favourable for an innovative drug, or more attention being given to preparation of the dossier for such products.

Authorisation under exceptional circumstances is a different issue. This is a facility whereby it is recognised that for certain diseases it is not possible to gather the same degree of efficacy data and thus a more limited file may be submitted. Whether this accelerates drug development or prevents the development of a particular drug being delayed is open to question.

A further variant on the procedures, the conditional licence, was introduced into European legislation with Commission Directive 91/507; it is also contained within the new centralised legislative procedure. This allows for a regulatory authority to license a product on more provisional data, provided the company completes studies to a satisfactory time-scale, with the authorisation being conditional upon satisfactory results. So far, competent authorities have been rather hesitant about this provision and there are also some doubts in industry circles. The argument raised is concerned with whether it is appropriate to authorise a product when there are still significant questions unanswered? Similarly, if an applicant is unable to complete the programme then are the conditions enforceable? It seems that conditional authorisation is being used, particularly at the Committee for Proprietary Medicinal Products (CPMP) level, to impose additional conditions rather than to accelerate the authorisation procedure. It may be of benefit if licensing is at an early stage based on surrogate markers where further data are required to verify those surrogates.

At this stage, therefore, there is little evidence to show that the need for the product is a determinant in the speed of the review or the time to bring the product to market.

Efficiency of regulatory authorities

Current regulatory performance

When looking at current performance and trends within regulatory authorities it is important to separate assessment performance from the overall time to market. Hence the response of industry as well as the response of regulatory agencies are pertinent. There is considerable variation in the time it takes industry to respond to similar questions both within the UK and at the European level.

The regulatory procedure worldwide is speeding up, as illustrated by data from the MCA (Figure 2.1). A 6-year analysis of assessment times, that is from receipt of the application to sign-off of the assessment report, for both new active substances and new chemical entities shows a very clear downward trend. This has continued into the first 6 months of 1995/96. Similar reductions have been seen in the area of abridged applications.

A number of factors have brought about this change within the MCA, including the introduction of more resources, adequate

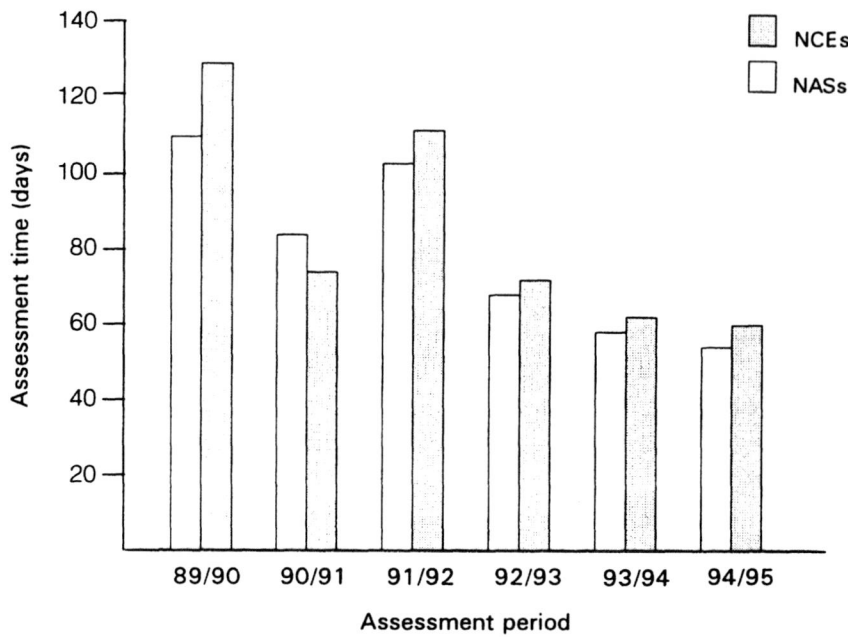

Figure 2.1 Average assessment times in the UK: 1989–1995

information technology (IT) and information systems (IS) support, management changes and initiatives, greater use of external experts, and recognition of the importance of dialogue. Since such improvements in assessment times are mirrored worldwide, there is now a greater challenge to industry to adequately plan and address all the scientific and development issues and then to provide high quality dossiers.

Worldwide review initiatives

A variety of initiatives are taking place across the regulatory authorities, as shown in Table 2.1. Dialogue on a national scale has been increasing. While not matching the degree of dialogue available with colleagues in the Food and Drug Administration (FDA), the UK has committed significant extra resource in this area. For many new

Table 2.1 Worldwide review initiatives

Dialogue
  during development
  during assessment
Production of concept papers/early guidelines
Electronic dossiers
IT/IS support
Mutual recognition/exchange of assessment reports
Training
Expert reports/process
External experts/independent advisory bodies

active substances, up to eight meetings will be held during the clinical trial phase through to approval, and open access will be available for talking through small issues on the telephone. Dialogue, however, needs careful planning, with recourse to experts to ensure correct information is provided. It may also necessitate stopping the regulatory time-clock to clarify issues. As with many initiatives there is a cost now with pay back later; within the European context the challenge is how to provide adequate resources for meaningful dialogue.

In the past, European guidelines have often been produced rather later. If there is a move towards the production of early guidelines to aid the pharmaceutical development process, regulators must ensure they do not inhibit science by fossilising thought. This can be achieved through concept papers which outline initial regulatory thinking for amplification at a later stage.

There is no convincing evidence that electronic dossiers accelerate the assessment process. However, they do help industry in the collection and assimilation of data, and in the applicants' response to regulatory questions. Electronic dossiers are a very real advantage to regulators. As we enter the era of the 500-volume dossier, with up to 100 volumes for abridged applications, they can provide important logistical gains in the storage and retrieval of data.

Adequate IT and IS support is fundamental as regulatory agencies move forward. This is particularly so in Europe where rapid and timely information flow is essential to support the system. Mutual recognition and exchange of assessment reports are equally important for authorities facing increased work volumes. There is no doubt that expert reports and the expert report process have added to the efficiency of assessments within Europe, while the use of external experts ensures appropriate regulation.

Other initiatives within Europe

The clear theme to the development of drug regulation in Europe has been one of co-operation and harmonisation between Member States. Much has been gained from the multistate procedure and the concertation procedure. Separate national assessments are giving way, through the new centralised and mutual recognition procedures, to shared work and increased efficiency, to accelerate the access of products across the European market. The International Conference on Harmonisation (ICH) process is welcomed as a move towards a common international data set. The voluntary Pharmaceutical Evaluation Report (PER) Scheme has demonstrated that the exchange of assessment reports between the 14 participating countries, facilitates regulatory approval of medicines worldwide.

Other short-term initiatives in Europe include development of assessment report guidelines, and training of assessors to ensure consistent and appropriate questions across the agencies. Regulatory quality assurance assumes increasing importance in an era where fewer authorities will be assessing the dossiers and the assessment process is faster. In the past the system of sequential licensing provided a degree of protection to the public health; moving to more rapid assessment in a larger market means more patients will be exposed to a potential hazard in the finite time before a particular pharmacovigilance problem can be identified. In this context the appointment of a rapporteur and co-rapporteur is welcomed to reduce the chance of a regulatory mistake. Finally, regulators must ensure they are asking relevant and appropriate questions to avoid product delays and increased costs. Both the CPMP and national agencies should pay attention to this issue.

Quality of dossier

Quality of data

It is well recognised that some dossiers are excellently presented and contain clearly assembled data; some, however, fall short of this. From a European perspective the expert report process is an important element here, bringing critical comment to a project at the earliest possible stage. Many believe this process needs to start when a candidate molecule enters Phase II, perhaps even earlier.

Undoubtedly, dialogue with regulators during development, particularly in the new European arrangement, will help improve the dossier, and regulatory authorities can further assist by providing feedback on dossiers and issuing new guidelines to highlight problems early.

It seems, however, that industry is losing sight of the purpose of the dossier. There are several elements to consider which include: resource document, integrated document, summary, critical analysis and history of the drug's development. The dossier is a resource document at the time of authorisation. It should also be an integrated document but all too often dossiers are compartmentalised; relationships between pharmaceutical, toxicological and clinical data are not addressed. Too frequently it seems to be forgotten that preclinical data is a stepping stone to clinical trials in humans. Equally, the very important lessons in comparative pharmacokinetics are not drawn out, or related to the Summary of Product Characteristics (SmPC) and other issues. Industry must break down the compartments and recognise that regulatory agencies assess the entire dossier.

In Europe we are not so interested in data but in the information that can be drawn out of the data. Regulatory agencies are overburdened with raw data which often submerges the significant message. The size of the clinical data base has remained static over 9 years, at just under 1500 patients evaluable for efficacy. However, the size of the dossier has increased ten-fold. To address this issue it is necessary to focus on the objectives of the perfect clinical dossier, which are set out below:

- To demonstrate efficacy in all indications within the proposed dosage regimens and with the formulation proposed for marketing;

- To provide reassurance on the safety in clinical usage;

- To produce an SmPC which fully reflects the dossier database and allows the product to be safely used.

Format/presentation of dossier

Experience within the MCA has shown that it can take three times longer to assess a poor quality dossier than an excellent one. Apart from the issues of format and presentation, the scientific development of the product should be considered. The MCA and other agencies have recommended drafting the SmPC as soon as a candidate molecule is recognised. This serves to identify clear objectives, even if the details of the SmPC are totally different at the end of development.

There is considerable variability in quality both within different parts of the dossier and within pharmaceutical corporations; clearly there is a need for quality assurance. Prioritisation of information and navigational aids greatly assist the reviewer.

Regulatory strategy

The importance of industry's regulatory strategy should not be overlooked in the context of improving drug regulation. Worldwide development clearly needs a corresponding regulatory strategy. The right decisions can make significant differences in the time to market. Such a strategy needs to be specific for the product, the company and the time frame; corporations need to have a clear objective of both the development and the commercialisation of the product.

Conclusion

The achievements in reducing time-lines for regulatory review have been impressive. The emphasis for the remainder of this decade will be to further reduce the overall time to market. This will require close co-operation between the regulators and the industry with increased dialogue during drug development, increased clarity of requirements for new products and increased co-operation between worldwide regulatory authorities. These concepts should come together in the improved quality of regulatory submissions and the improved quality of the regulatory process.

References

Rawlins MD and Jefferys DB (1991). Study of the UK Product Licence Applications containing new active substances 1987–9. *British Medical Journal*, **302**: 233–235.

Lund I and Dukes MNG (1980). Les répercussions du control administratif des médicaments étude de la situation en Norvège et aux Pays Bas. *Industrie Santé*, **49**: 37–57.

3 Company strategies to ensure a quick and efficient review: A biotech company

RALPH SMALLING

Summary

1. The first way to speed the review process is to develop a good working relationship with the regulatory authorities. While taking advantage of all opportunities for meetings with the regulators, no dialogue should be without purpose.

2. Constructing a worldwide licensing strategy which recognises differences in regulatory requirements in the major regions will facilitate both product development and regulatory review. For the technically complex biotechnology industry, continuity of staff and international involvement of the same development team will also be of value.

3. Manufacturing issues can, and do, delay licensure. It is important to finalise manufacturing processes for biotechnology products prior to Phase III studies, since process changes thereafter may alter the end product. There are unique constraints on the manufacture of biologics. Any contractual agreements should be written so as not to create impossible regulatory hurdles.

4. A well-organised submission that is easy to read will aid review, and in-house quality assurance should ensure the dossier is well assembled. Proactive planning to anticipate regulatory concerns can speed response to questions.

5.   Regulatory initiatives around the world, including the Prescription Drug User Fee Act (PDUFA), the International Conference on Harmonisation (ICH), memoranda of understanding (MOU) and the establishment of the Committee for Proprietary Medicinal Products (CPMP) procedure in Europe, are helping to advance the review process.

Introduction

The review and approval of a new pharmaceutical is a complex undertaking which involves a number of inter-related factors and activities. Lack of attention in any area can cause delays in time of approval. The process really begins prior to initiating clinical trials and continues through the filing and review of the marketing application. There are several means by which a company can increase its chances for a quick and efficient review of its regulatory submissions. These are addressed in the following sections from the perspective of a biotechnology company which has rapidly progressed from start-up to a mature company with international operations.

Relationships with regulatory authorities

The first, rather obvious, point is for the company to establish good working relations with the regulatory authorities at the earliest opportunity. For companies working in the United States, this process can begin before submission of the first Investigational New Drug (IND) application with a request for a pre-IND meeting to discuss the product under development.

Bringing a drug through development and review is a lengthy, arduous process which should be seen as a co-operative effort involving a partnership between the company and the regulatory authority. The company should take advantage of all meeting opportunities, such as pre-Phase III and pre-licensing meetings; dialogue with regulatory authorities is to be encouraged. That said, however, contacts with regulatory authorities should be of appropriate frequency to assure active flow of information and discussion of issues, and not frivolous or without purpose.

It is wise to thoroughly prepare for all interactions with regulatory agencies, since these are valuable commodities which companies often wish could occur more frequently. When such meetings are granted, a company should maximise their value by providing a well-organised and concise pre-meeting package containing a clear agenda. Prior to the meeting, the company should rehearse thoroughly; conference calls should be treated with similar preparation.

In this way issues can be addressed as they arise, rather than waiting for filing (when they may slow the review process).

Worldwide licensing strategy

A worldwide licensing strategy can be developed by researching and understanding the differences in regulatory requirements in the major marketing regions; this will speed the entire development and review process. Since developing products derived from biotechnology frequently involve technically complex issues, ensuring continuity of personnel assigned to a project and involving discovery and process development scientists through to submission often pays dividends. Similarly, using the same development team internationally can bring continuity to the application process and facilitate internal communication, thus potentially speeding the review process.

Companies must have a candid awareness of their product's strengths and weaknesses and of shortcomings in the regulatory application. Within Europe, expert reports prepared for the marketing application should truly represent "critical" analysis, and not a "cheerleading" exercise. Finalisation of the reports should involve all experts together (or at least the clinical and toxicology experts), as the data developed in each area should inter-relate and support each other.

The cost of developing a new pharmaceutical product has traditionally been high, but has risen even more dramatically in recent years. Financing the effort is a daunting task for young biotechnology companies, and often partnerships with large established firms are sought. Care should be taken in the choice of partners and the terms of the agreement. Contractual language should not create impossible regulatory hurdles, or define responsibilities that are not possible under existing regulations. This has been a particular issue for biotechnology companies whose products are regulated as biologics, where current regulations dictate that the final manufacturer is the licence holder.

Clinical data undoubtedly form the corner-stone of any marketing application; any deficiency in the trial design and statistical analysis will inevitably affect the efficiency of the review. The Food and Drug Administration (FDA) has set a goal of auditing 50% of data included in New Drug Applications (NDAs)/Product Licence Applications (PLAs). Therefore the quality of clinical data must be assured through well-designed protocols, studies conducted in accordance with established Good Clinical Practices, and thorough monitoring and adequate preparation of each site for an FDA inspection.

Facility/manufacturing issues

Growing biotechnology companies often lack the facilities or the finances to build the manufacturing plants which are optimal for introduction of the product onto the market. In addition, the need for companies to reach the market quickly often means that manufacturing processes are not optimised early and improvements are continually sought. In addition, the nature of biotechnology products often means the manufacturing process is technically complex; changing the manufacturing process may change the end product. A strong emphasis should therefore be placed on finalising the process prior to initiation of Phase III studies, and one should exercise significant resistance to making changes thereafter.

A pre-licence inspection will occur during the review process. The advantages of rigorous preparation for this event cannot be overemphasised. Manufacturing issues can, and do, delay licensure. Small companies which consider contracting out selected manufacturing steps, such as fill and finish, should adopt a "hands-on" approach by positioning one of their own staff to work in the plant. Similarly, if outside contractors are used to validate the production facility, the company should be actively involved in the process. Biologics regulations put unique constraints on such manufacturing arrangements.

The marketing application

Poor submissions have a great impact on the review process. Companies should develop a well-organised, "user-friendly" application that is easy to read, appropriately tabbed and professionally styled (proper margins, legible font, etc.). To this end, details such as pagination, table of contents, and format requirements in different countries must be taken into account. A quality assurance step within the application development process will ensure the application is well assembled. Submission of an electronic data package is an option; it is important to discuss any such plans with the appropriate agencies well in advance.

In assessing the application's strengths and weaknesses, it is wise to anticipate regulatory concerns. By developing a proactive plan to address these, questions from the agencies can receive a speedy response.

Regulatory initiatives

A number of regulatory initiatives to improve the review process are either in effect or in the process of development. In the United States one of the major initiatives has been the Prescription Drug User Fee Act (PDUFA) enacted in 1992. This Act was designed to make funds available to the FDA for recruiting additional review staff in order to speed approvals, and it imposes time constraints on the FDA for application reviews. However, the time constraints require only that an action be taken, which can range from final approval to generation of a non-approvable letter. As no constraints are imposed on the time to a final decision, reviews can still extend indefinitely. That said, the Act has appeared to focus attention on review times, and although it is still early, seems to be having a positive impact (Table 3.1). For example, the FDA has been successful in addressing the backlog of applications exceeding the statutory 180-day action clock and has been meeting its goals with regard to acting upon applications. The number of amendments received by the FDA has been reduced and, most importantly, the number of major amendments (which extend the review clock) has been significantly reduced. The number of refusals-to-file has also been reduced, which either means that industry is improving its applications or is becoming more cautious. The FDA is certainly making strides in hiring additional review-related staff to handle the influx of applications.

Table 3.1 Impact of the US Prescription Drug User Fee Act (PDUFA)

Goal	*Status*
Elimination of backlog of drug applications exceeding the 180-day statutory action clock	Action on the last of the nearly 700 overdue submissions should have been undertaken by July 1995 (F-D-C Reports, Vol. 56, No. 50, pp. 3–4, 12/12/94)
Initiate regulatory action within 12 months on incoming efficacy and manufacturing supplements	For financial year 1994, FDA projected that 44% of efficacy supplements and 65% of manufacturing supplements will have met this goal (F-D-C Reports, Vol. 56, No. 50, pp. 3–4, 12/12/94)
Reduce the number of amendments received by FDA during review of licence applications	For financial year 1994, 77% of NDA submissions reviewed to the point of FDA action have not included major amendments; 59% had no minor amendments during the same review period (F-D-C Reports, Vol. 56, No. 50, pp. 3–4, 12/12/94)
Reduce the percentage of applications subjected to FDA refusal-to-file	For CBER in financial year 1994, 38% of applications were refused for filing, were considered unacceptable for filing, or were withdrawn by applicants before filing. Early data for 1995 show no similar actions (Biologics and Biotech Report, 2/95)
Recruit 300 additional Center for Drug Evaluation and Research/Center for Biologics Evaluation and Research review staff in first quarter of the 1995 financial year	On target. As of 1st October 1994, FDA had recruited 645 review-related staff, resulting in a net gain of 272 review staff (F-D-C Reports, Vol. 56, No. 50, pp. 3–4, 12/12/94)

International harmonisation of regulations has significant potential as a mechanism by which reviews can be hastened. The ICH process has helped in specific areas such as product quality and toxicity testing, but as yet has not dealt with the broader issues of regional differences in data requirements, which are more difficult to address. If the expectations of international regulatory agencies are indeed harmonised, the goal of achieving truly global registration packages moves closer. The likely benefit would be fewer questions as a result of the idiosyncrasies of different authorities.

Other initiatives all fall under a general heading of mutual co-operation. For example, the United States has a memorandum of understanding (MOU) with various countries to recognise the inspection of foreign manufacturing facilities. In Amgen's experience the MOU existing between Canada, Sweden and Australia regarding mutual recognition of a shared procedure shortened the review process for filgastrim. Experience in Europe with the CPMP procedure was also positive, to the extent that it allowed for an expedient review and approval in a number of countries almost simultaneously.

Although generally supportive of the concept of accelerated or special review processes, it is Amgen's experience that it may be difficult for a biotechnology company to take advantage of these initiatives. Accelerated review processes are based on surrogate endpoints; for biotechnology products it is hard to identify accepted surrogate endpoints when the diseases in question are not well understood.

Conclusion

Ultimately, both industry and regulatory agencies should be aware of the challenges facing all of us. The number of biotechnology product candidates is increasing rapidly and will accelerate as the human genome is further decoded and other scientific advances are made. However, since resources available for developing human therapeutics are limited, innovative approaches are required to ensure that safe and efficacious therapeutics become available to patients in an expeditious way and at reasonable cost.

Reference

Prescription Drug User Fee Act (PDUFA) (1992). United States Goverment Public Law #102-571, October 29, 1992.

4 Company strategies to ensure a quick and efficient review: A Japanese company

BRAM MORGENSTERN

Summary

1. Traditionally, Japanese companies have licensed their new products to US and European pharmaceutical companies. Since development programmes primarily addressed Japanese medical practices and regulatory requirements, the need for additional work for other markets resulted in long development times in other territories.

2. The globalisation and integration of an organisation, with synchronised development of new products between Japan, Europe and the USA should avoid duplication, improve the quality of the dossier, and reduce development time and costs.

3. There are a number of steps in the regulatory process where cultural and practical issues, such as language, attitude towards "authority" and organisational structure, can present difficulties to a Japanese company trying to operate on a worldwide basis.

Introduction

An important element in a company's strategy to ensure minimal review time is the company's effort to provide a registration dossier of sufficient quality. This means that the company's development programme should be designed to provide sufficient information to enable the regulatory authorities to establish the efficacy and safety of the product. This paper will focus on the globalisation of development from the perspective of a Japanese pharmaceutical company and consider where cultural and practical issues may affect aspects of the review process.

Globalisation of the development programme

Worldwide, the development times of new products are lengthening due to increasing knowledge about disease mechanisms, wider possibilities of experimentation and more stringent regulatory requirements. For many years Japanese pharmaceutical companies concentrated their research and development, manufacturing and marketing activities on the Japanese and, to some extent, other Asian markets. The larger Japanese companies licensed their new products to US and European pharmaceutical companies who then, rather independently, developed the products for their licensed territories. After registration the licensees commercialised the products, frequently under their own name, without much public awareness of the Japanese originator. Some Japanese companies established business offices in the USA and European countries to liaise between their licensees and the Japanese headquarters.

Usually, original Japanese development programmes addressed primarily domestic medical practices and regulatory requirements. Consequently the additional development programmes for Europe and the USA were extensive and time-consuming, and led to long total development times. The mix of data generated in the various territories, sometimes with considerable differences in control regimes and timepoints of performance, could be detrimental to the quality of the dossier.

Until the early 1990s, the activities of Yamanouchi Pharmaceutical Company Limited (Tokyo) in the ethical pharmaceutical markets of Europe and the USA were based on this "classical" strategy of licensing with small local business/development units. To cope with the changing environment of the pharmaceutical industry, Yamanouchi adopted a strategy of becoming a global enterprise engaged in worldwide R&D, manufacturing and marketing activities through integrated business organisations covering Asia, Europe and the USA. Yamanouchi is now the only Japanese pharmaceutical company with an extensive European organisation, and is therefore not a "typical example" of a Japanese pharmaceutical company doing worldwide business.

By globalising its development activities, Yamanouchi aims to synchronise the development of new products in the three main territories and thereby, in particular, to avoid duplication, to improve quality of the dossier and to reduce development time and costs (Figure 4.1).

Cultural aspects

In analysing Yamanouchi's, still limited, experience with the regulatory review process outside Japan, it is worthwhile considering some cultural aspects which influence communications between parties and how the Japanese company may experience the process (Table 4.1).

Communication between Japanese and non-Japanese is hampered by the difficulties of learning to write and speak each other's language. Access to the original Japanese R&D database is open only to Japanese-speaking staff. This makes compilation of the dossier, and also obtaining quick answers to questions, difficult for the subsidiary company. Reviewers should be aware that study reports translated from Japanese may not be perfect, and be prepared to use the telephone to request clarification from the applicant.

Strict compliance with regulations and instructions from regulatory authorities is essential in Japan. Objections to, and criticism of, the dossier are taken very personally by the Japanese R&D scientists.

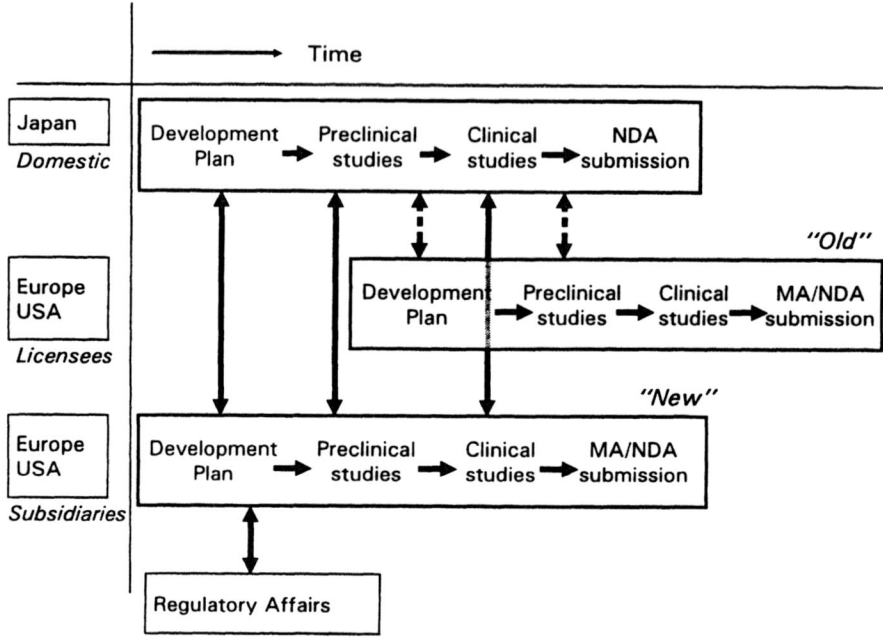

Figure 4.1 Global synchronisation of development

In Europe there may be more room for contradiction and/or discussion, sometimes through direct confrontation. This approach is not familiar to the Japanese. Requests to a Japanese company for additional studies during the review process and also in pre-submission consultations should be well explained and reasoned to avoid unnecessary animal and human studies.

The organisation of Japanese pharmaceutical companies may differ considerably from that of European and/or US companies. In large Japanese companies there are several layers of hierarchy which may not be easily identified by an organisation diagram. Decision-making is based on consensus which requires considerable time. To contact the right person for the right answer requires understanding of the internal informal organisation structure. Skilful liaison staff should be available to achieve efficient communication.

Table 4.1 Japan–Europe: differences of cultural nature influencing regulatory strategies

- Language – communication
  – access to Japanese database
  – translations

- Attitude towards "authority" – compliance
  – acceptance of criticism
  – contradiction and discussion
  – challenging and negotiation

- Organisation of Japanese company
  – decision making process
  – "informal" organisation

Regulatory review process

Pre-submission consultation

In the design of a global development programme it is essential to obtain sufficient insight into the "European view" about what is required. This is not easy to achieve, particularly for a Japanese company. On the one hand, as the Committee for Proprietary Medicinal Products (CPMP) guidelines are comprised of different Member State opinions they often lack specificity, and are frequently poly-interpretable. On the other hand, the European Union is often seen in Japan as the "United States of Europe", and the European Medicines Evaluation Agency (EMEA) as a federal European FDA. The differences in product and dossier assessments in different Member States are poorly understood in Japan.

The influences of different medical practices, different scientific "schools", political and economic reasoning or just lack of sufficient expertise and staff, still lead to different regulatory assessments in the Member States notwithstanding 30 years of harmonisation. Maybe there is a need for "European Advisory Committees". If a "European view" cannot be identified, the global development programme may be exclusively based on input from the Ministry of

Health and Welfare (MHW) and Food and Drug Administration (FDA) consultations.

Dossier content issues

GMP and GLP standards in Japan are comparable to European and US standards. Manufacturing and control data, as well as preclinical study results, generated in Japan should therefore be acceptable to regulatory authorities outside Japan. Clinical studies in Japan must be assessed on a case-by-case basis as to whether they can contribute to European/US submissions. Differences in metabolism due to race appear not to occur to a degree that is often suggested. However, differences in dose regimen do occur and this tends to complicate matters.

Critical evaluation and identification of weaknesses as is required in an expert report are only reluctantly accepted by Japanese R&D staff. The new instructions about separating the factual summary part and a critical evaluation part may be more acceptable and may require less discussion in the preparatory phase.

Outcome of regulatory review

The experience of Yamanouchi with simultaneous submissions, relating to one drug, in six EU Member States (all with reputable evaluation experience in multistate and Pharmaceutical Evaluation Report Scheme (PER) procedures) is summarised in Table 4.2. This shows the variability in the number of requests for clarification/further information in three sections of the dossier.

The formulation of objections and questions should be as specific as possible. Release of a copy of the assessment report together with the list of objections, as is done by the UK, the Netherlands and Sweden, is extremely helpful in providing background information and the necessary detail. The willingness of several regulatory authorities in the EU to allow a more or less formal verbal discussion on the objections, as experienced in our latest submissions, is a

Table 4.2 NCE assessment in six Member States (three full-scale assessment reports received)

	Clarification/further information requested
Chemistry and pharmacy section	
Validation report of active ingredient analysis	1 of 6
Microbiological purity	2 of 6
Tightening of limits of total impurities	2 of 6
GMP certificate	1 of 6
Human pharmacology and clinical data	
Effects of renal insufficiency	3 of 6
Pharmacokinetics and safety in the "elderly"	3 of 6
Long-term efficacy and safety	6 of 6
Questioning optimal dose	2 of 6
Questions related to clinical trials reported as "ongoing"	3 of 6
Changes proposed to SmPC	2 of 6
Pharmacotoxicology	
Finding about male fertility in SmPC	1 of 6
Extension of table format of carcinogenicity study results	1 of 6
Three more mutagenicity studies	1 of 6
Questions about findings in carcinogenicity studies	2 of 6

significant step forward in achieving a reduced and more efficient review time.

SmPC/Labelling

As in most large pharmaceutical companies, the text of the Summary of Product Characteristics (SmPC) or labelling is under supervision by, or needs approval by, the company's headquarters. The use of more than one language (English) during the regulatory review process in the European mutual recognition or centralised procedures during the period of negotiation, is detrimental to the speed and efficiency of regulatory review. It is my personal opinion that in the mutual recognition procedure, harmonisation of the SmPC text between Member States should be restricted to the most important paragraphs of the SmPC, allowing Member States to adapt to national style, and medical practices, and to take into account competitor product SmPCs.

Quality assurance

In Japan a great deal of emphasis is placed on quality control procedures with respect to content, in order to achieve consistency throughout the dossier. Equally, assessment reports of regulatory authorities should be subject to quality assurance procedures, as each report is supposed to present a balanced judgement on the basis of generally accepted scientific standards.

Conclusion

In conclusion, the globalisation and integration of an organisation should lead to reduced development times. However, there are a number of steps in the regulatory process where cultural and practical issues can present difficulties to a Japanese company trying to operate on a worldwide basis.

5 Company strategies to ensure a quick and efficient review: A transnational company

EMILY DONNELLY, JAMES RITCHIE and
STEVEN FRENCH

Summary

1. The speed and efficiency of new drug approval is a key determinant of the continued success of the pharmaceutical industry. This paper describes the approach taken by a company with a transnational structure to facilitate quick and efficient regulatory reviews.

2. Whilst overall drug development times are too long and are increasing, by setting challenging but achievable targets, submission time has been reduced remarkably and approval time cut, although various issues outside industry control have prevented the latter target being fully achieved.

3. Process improvement initiatives can pay large dividends in reducing cycle times, increasing efficiency and cutting costs. Within the regulatory process these require traditional organisational company boundaries to be ignored.

4. Regulatory intelligence and know-how, combined with regulatory strategy and planning, are vital in utilising information effectively and ensuring that the complex process from drug development to approval is well managed.

5. There are many opportunities for agency/industry communications; these should be managed effectively. The key to progress is partnership. A partnership approach could have a significant impact upon both the speed and efficiency of the review process.

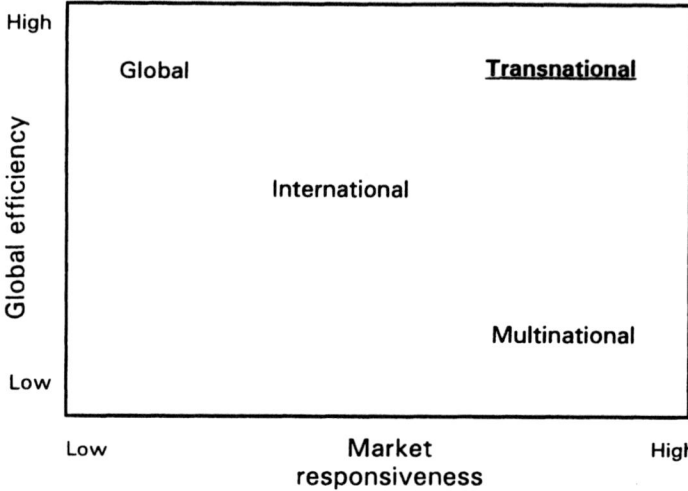

Figure 5.1 The corporate organisational challenge. Based on work by Bartlett and Ghoshal (1987a, b and 1989)

The corporate organisational challenge

The joint imperatives of high global efficiency and high market responsiveness are redefining how large corporations should be organised, since neither a "Global" organisational structure, nor organisation on a "Multinational" basis, fully satisfies the requirements of the current global environment. A "Transnational" structure is designed to meet these challenges, through ensuring the delivery of high levels of global efficiency whilst retaining maximum customer focus (Figure 5.1).

It used to be the case that the pharmaceutical industry was characterised by high margins and year on year organic growth. This is no longer certain. As economic and competitive forces intensify on the industry, so the speed and efficiency of new drug approval is a key determinant of continued success. It is clear that industry can, and must, have a major impact in this area. Many initiatives have already had a positive influence on review times, but opportunities exist for further progress, particularly in the area of joint industry/agency initiatives.

This paper describes the approach of a transnational company (SmithKline Beecham) has taken in facilitating quick and efficient regulatory reviews, thereby ensuring the timely availability of valuable new medicines to patients, and an appropriate and legitimate return on investment for the company.

Reducing review times – focus areas

SmithKline Beecham (SB) has pursued a broad range of initiatives focusing on five areas with an impact on review times:

- Definition of overall targets (objectives)
- Process improvement
- Regulatory intelligence and know-how
- Regulatory strategy and planning
- Communications

Definition of targets

By defining overall targets (objectives) one can drive performance. The impact of first setting challenging targets (Figure 5.2) and then constantly improving them can be clearly seen by the startling improvements achieved by SmithKline Beecham in submission and approval times during the period 1987 to 1995 (Figure 5.3).

Prior to 1990, submission time (defined as "time from submission in first market to submission in eighth market") in the eight major markets could be as long as 7 years. This was primarily because multinational organisations normally developed and registered medicines independently country by country. When a global standard was established and development co-ordinated on a global basis, it then became possible to reduce submission time to 6 months which was a target established at the time of the merger between Beecham and SmithKline Beckman (1989). Finally, this submission time was reduced to 7 days in 1995 and a long-term target remains of 24 hours. Such a narrow window for submission automatically helps to ensure early approvals, minimises rework, ensures consistency of message

---

Scope: *Development time*

	Target
Advice during development	Deliverence of advice never rate-limiting on development
Time from last patient last visit to submission	3 months

Scope: *Time to submission and approval in 10 major markets*

	Target
Submission time (time from submission in first market to submission in tenth market)	1 week
Approval time (time for submission in first market to approval in tenth market)	18 months

---

Figure 5.2 Examples of targets

to the regulatory agencies and simplifies the management processes, i.e. global efficiency.

Whereas submission time is entirely within the company's control, approval time is greatly dependent on effective regulatory authority systems. However, company focus on approval time can pay tremendous dividends. Approval time (defined as "the time from submission in the first market to approval in the eighth market") pre-1990 in the eight major markets was up to 9 years. At the time of the merger, the target time of 4 years was established and this target has now been decreased to 18 months in 1995. This has been achieved by optimising regulatory strategy and proactively networking with regulatory authorities to allow faster review. Quicker approval time enables an organisation to maximise its assets and provide greater flexibility in terms of launch plans and improved patent protection. Fast approval is only possible if the file is customer-focused to the particular market, i.e. market responsiveness.

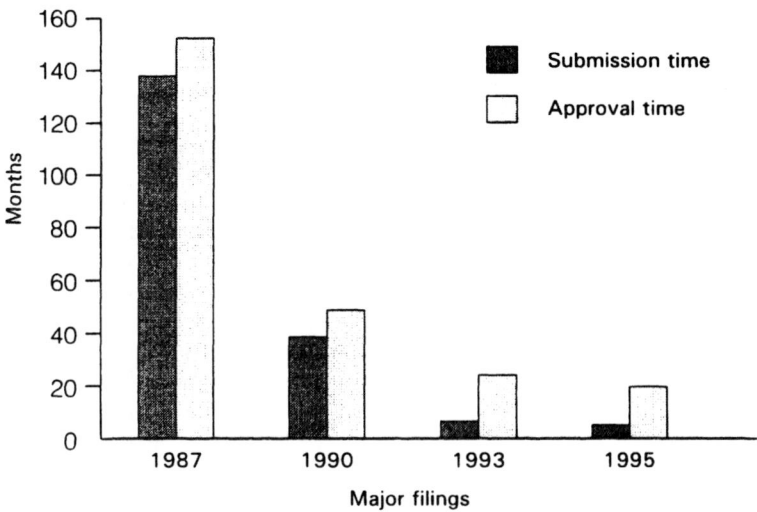

Figure 5.3 Major filings – submissions and approval times in 24 developed markets

Although great strides have been made, issues outside company control in relation to specific regulatory procedures continue to prevent full achievement of the desired targets. In particular, in Canada and Germany, line extensions cannot be filed until the initial file is approved. In Japan the need for separate clinical development, together with the requirement to complete clinical development before filing the submission, can cause significant obstacles. In addition, the proposed mutual recognition system in Europe is considered to present a number of major difficulties. The requirement for approval in a first market followed by sequential approvals, with the possibility of objections, offers a serious threat to corporate aspirations in terms of approval time.

Process improvement initiatives

Improvement areas within pharmaceutical new product development can be identified by systematically documenting the overall process before targeting specific critical path activities where

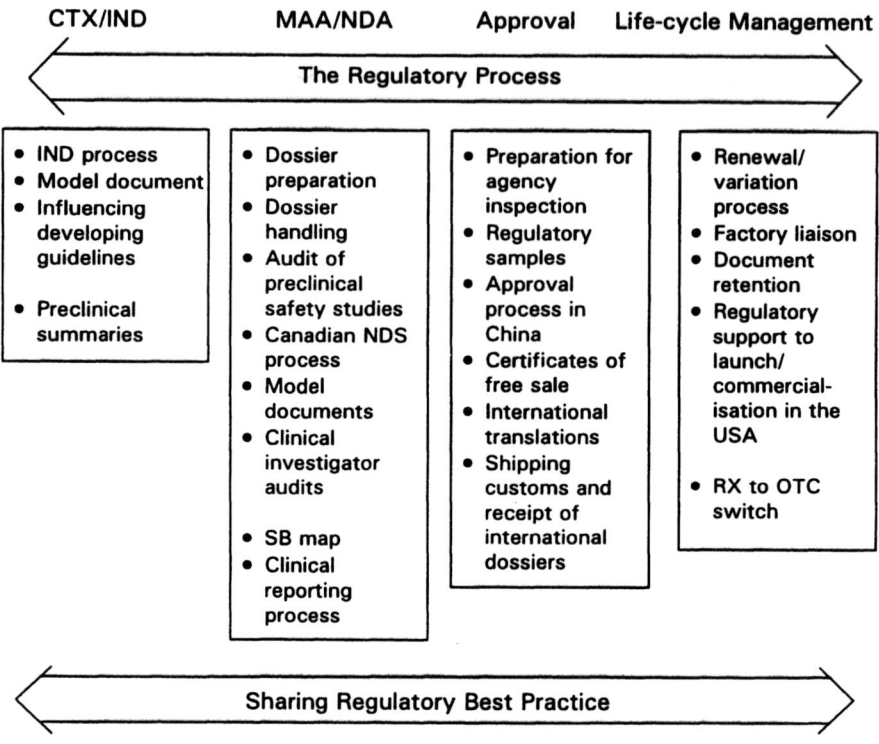

CTX, Clinical trial exemption; IND, investigational new drug; MAA, marketing authorisation application; NDA, new drug application

Figure 5.4 Process improvement initiatives

detailed analysis and measurement can be undertaken. Industry experience demonstrates that process improvement can pay large dividends in reducing cycle time, increasing efficiency and reducing costs. Application of process improvement tools and techniques to the process of drug development has also resulted in higher quality, more focused and user friendly regulatory dossiers and ultimately faster reviews.

Process improvement projects can also be applied within the regulatory function (Figure 5.4), including cross-functional process activities. By analogy, application of these concepts across the industry/agency interface could produce significant improvements in regulatory systems.

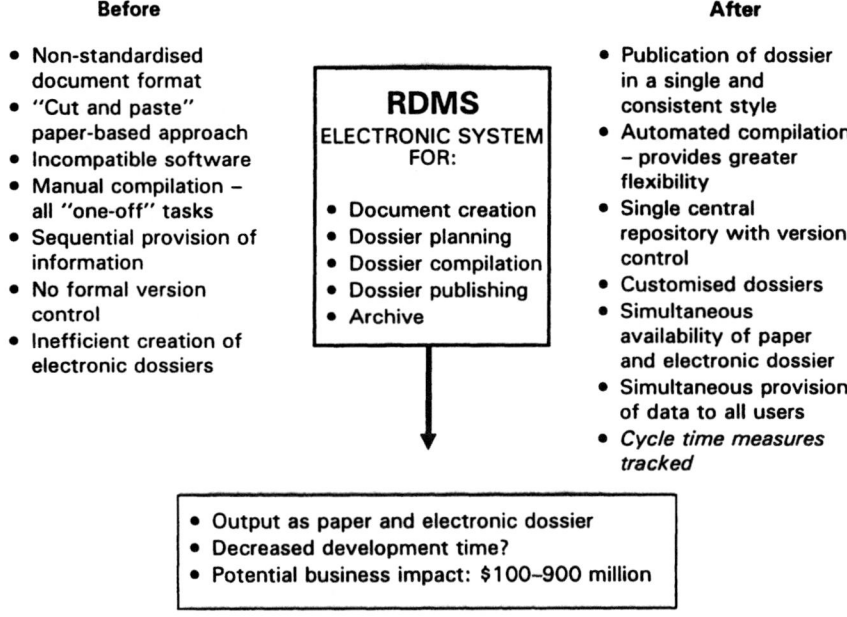

Before

- Non-standardised document format
- "Cut and paste" paper-based approach
- Incompatible software
- Manual compilation – all "one-off" tasks
- Sequential provision of information
- No formal version control
- Inefficient creation of electronic dossiers

RDMS

ELECTRONIC SYSTEM FOR:

- Document creation
- Dossier planning
- Dossier compilation
- Dossier publishing
- Archive

After

- Publication of dossier in a single and consistent style
- Automated compilation – provides greater flexibility
- Single central repository with version control
- Customised dossiers
- Simultaneous availability of paper and electronic dossier
- Simultaneous provision of data to all users
- *Cycle time measures tracked*

- Output as paper and electronic dossier
- Decreased development time?
- Potential business impact: $100–900 million

Figure 5.5 Regulatory Document Management System (RDMS)

The objective of one SB initiative was to develop an efficient process allowing timely submission of dossiers worldwide. The one week target, from receipt of core dossier to submission in key markets, was achieved. The impact of quicker submission (<5 days in five major markets) for a recent marketing authorisation, could result in additional revenue in excess of £10 million. This illustrates how the targeting of a particular process has paved the way for considerable potential benefits.

A second internal process improvement project entailed the fundamental redesign of a process to significantly change the way work is done (Figure 5.5). The new Regulatory Document Management System (RDMS) provides simultaneous paper and electronic dossiers in a standardised format; the potential financial impact is considerable.

Regulatory intelligence and know-how

Thorough knowledge of regulatory systems, requirements, precedents and procedures will improve the quality of a dossier and the efficiency of a review. However, regulatory intelligence and know-how is more than just knowing the guidelines, it requires the ability to capture, process and effectively utilise information from numerous sources. A company can develop a centre of excellence which can provide up-to-date regulatory information and optional strategies to project teams. Undoubtedly, the capacity for the organisation to learn is very important; the rapid transfer of best practice is a major source of competitive advantage in this area.

Regulatory strategy and planning

Regulatory strategy and planning are vital in ensuring that the complex process from drug development to approval is well managed and aligned with worldwide regulatory authority expectations. Clear targets, in terms of well defined indications and target labelling, must be set and supported by a development plan in line with all available regulatory intelligence. The plan must be a living document that is continuously tested and modified throughout its life, in keeping with changes in the regulatory environment. A key factor can be advice from regulatory authorities during development. This should be planned for, sought at the appropriate time, and then used to modify the development plan when appropriate. The resulting development plan, which is robust in regulatory terms, will ensure a faster and more efficient review.

Communications

There are many opportunities for agency/industry communication during the development process, during review and in the post-approval phase. Effective management of such opportunities is vital in ensuring that communications assist rather than hinder the review process. To develop a close, effective and efficient working relationship, industry should maximise its communications expertise using a range of media (written, oral, new technologies). Above all, industry must be "customer-focused" in its communications, that is, well prepared, timely and not time-wasting, honest, open and professional. Communications must be concise, well judged and competent while reflecting sensitivity and cultural awareness.

Agencies increasingly have a role and responsibility to participate in initiatives to increase the quality and effectiveness of industry/ agency interactions, particularly in the area of technological compatibility and standardisation. The key to progress is partnership.

The partnership approach

A traditionalist view of the interface between industry and authorities was that industry developed drugs, then, once development was complete, the information was handed to the authorities for review. A more enlightened view may be described as a "partnership approach" whereby industry and the regulators have a close but well defined working relationship throughout the life-cycle of a drug to assist the regulatory review process. Reservations concerning an "over-cosy" relationship between the partners are not well founded and can be addressed.

Industry experience has shown that the setting and review of joint targets – in the areas of review time, advice during development, or time for labelling approval, will drive towards quicker reviews. Clear, accessible guidance on labelling (e.g. can comparative clinical data be included?), for instance, would reduce ambiguity, minimise resource requirements and permit more rapid approval of applications. Finally, a joint approach to the training of employees would be beneficial to both the agencies and industry by raising overall standards, and so developing a pool of more informed and capable regulatory professionals.

The many opportunities from such a "partnership approach" could collectively have a significant impact upon both the speed and efficiency of the review process and be to the mutual benefit of both parties (Figure 5.6). Administrative information could be filed

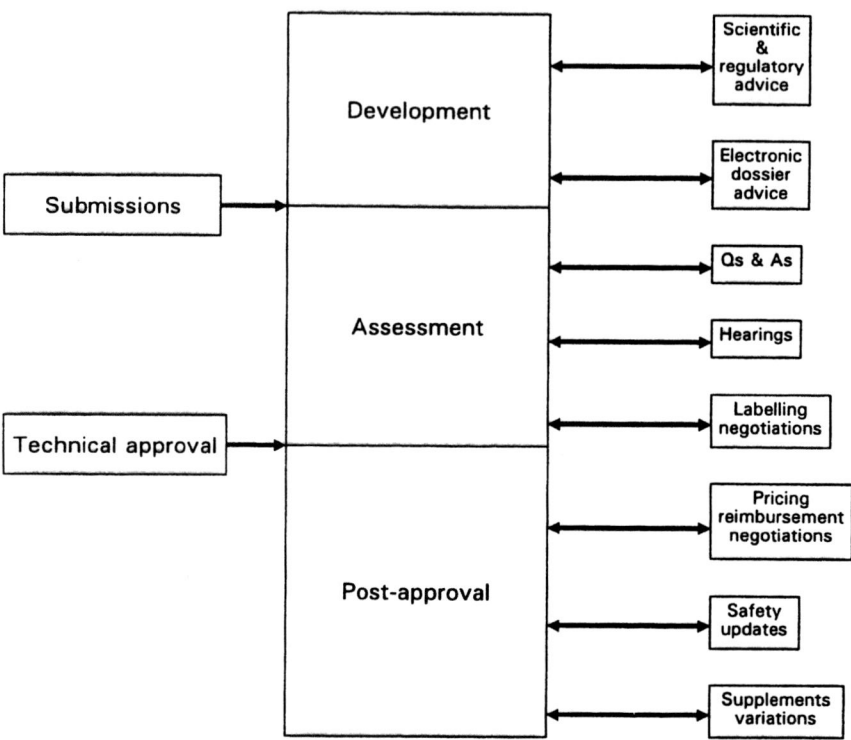

Figure 5.6 Agency/industry communication opportunities

electronically with authorities, while product licence information could be held in databases and be maintained "on-line", with suitable accessibility for both the drug regulatory agency and the licence-holder. Conditional approvals could be more widely used where minor issues can be resolved readily and it should be possible to submit and process applications independently from one another, so that delays caused by the need for sequential filing are removed. For their part, industry could assist agencies in their workload planning, by indicating in advance the number of future applications or through resource analysis and planning techniques. A flexible approach to safety updates (i.e. recognising the efficiencies in generating synchronised worldwide safety updates) by the authorities would greatly assist industry, as would some form of continuous assessment (rolling review). Finally, joint process improvement initiatives could be pursued to help achieve joint targets with in-built integrity.

Conclusion

There is much that has been done by both industry and regulatory agencies to improve the speed and efficiency of drug reviews. A transnational company's multifaceted approach has included setting and striving to achieve appropriate targets, process definition and improvement, and emphasis on regulatory know-how, strategy and communications. However, there is still more that can be done.

There is opportunity for greater partnership between the pharmaceutical industry and its regulators working together to facilitate the availability of medicines of appropriate safety, quality and efficacy as rapidly as is commensurate with the protection of public health, thereby delivering maximum benefit to all stakeholders in our regulatory systems.

References

Bartlett CA and Ghoshal S (1987a). Managing across borders: new strategic requirements. *Sloan Management Review*, Summer, 7–17.

Bartlett CA and Ghoshal S (1987b). Managing across borders: new organization responses. *Sloan Management Review*, Fall, 45–53.

Bartlett CA and Ghoshal S (1989). *Managing across Borders: the Transnational Solution*. Century Business, London, pp. 274.

6 Conditional licensing: Advantages and disadvantages

MARIA HOLZ-SLOMCZYK and
ALFRED G HILDEBRANDT

Summary

1. The legal requirements and issues regarding the conditional approval of pharmaceuticals, before they have undergone full and adequate testing, vary from country to country.

2. In the USA, three special situations allow the use of a product outside the investigational new drug (IND) protocol, during pre-approval clinical testing. In addition it is possible to expedite the development and approval process, in specific circumstances.

3. Within the EU centralised procedure, early approval may be granted "under exceptional circumstances" with the results of further studies being required within a specified time period.

4. The German Drug Law allows the granting of a provisional authorisation when it is in the public interest to introduce a product onto the market immediately. The requirements and procedures for conditional approvals in Germany are discussed.

5. The provisional authorisation of products for life-threatening conditions is largely advocated by most parties involved. However, for both ethical and scientific reasons, concerns have been expressed. There is a need for discussion between all parties concerning the level of proof of efficacy and safety needed before conditional approval is granted.

Introduction

Medical products are usually placed on the market after thorough testing of safety, efficacy and quality. This paper deals with those preparations that have not undergone full and adequate testing, which are however of so great, or at least presumed, value that they justify privileged placing on the market.

As a rule, quality, safety and efficacy of a product must be proven, in order to obtain a marketing authorisation. However, there is the possibility that quality and safety of a product are proven and that there is a reasonable assumption of efficacy which can be substantiated by further data after authorisation.

The legal requirements and issues with regard to the approval of pharmaceuticals which are not sufficiently tested differ from country to country. Fast-track approval, conditional licensing and an increased readiness of the regulatory authorities to dialogue with the industry, are new regulatory concepts in many countries (Figure 6.1).

USA

During clinical testing under investigational new drug status (IND), the Food and Drug Administration (FDA) allows use of the drug in three special situations outside the IND protocol (Mathieu, 1990; Nightingale, 1994). These are: the so-called compassionate or single patient IND, the treatment IND, the parallel-track policy, the accelerated approval and Subpart E procedures.

Compassionate use

Compassionate use of investigational new drugs has been permitted by the FDA since the 1950s in order to assure that individual patients, who have no other alternative, are not denied any promising treatment. This term is used to describe the release of a drug, usually on a single-patient basis, outside of a study environment and refers to a variety of informal, extra-regulatory mechanisms under which experimental, off-market, and otherwise unapproved drugs are

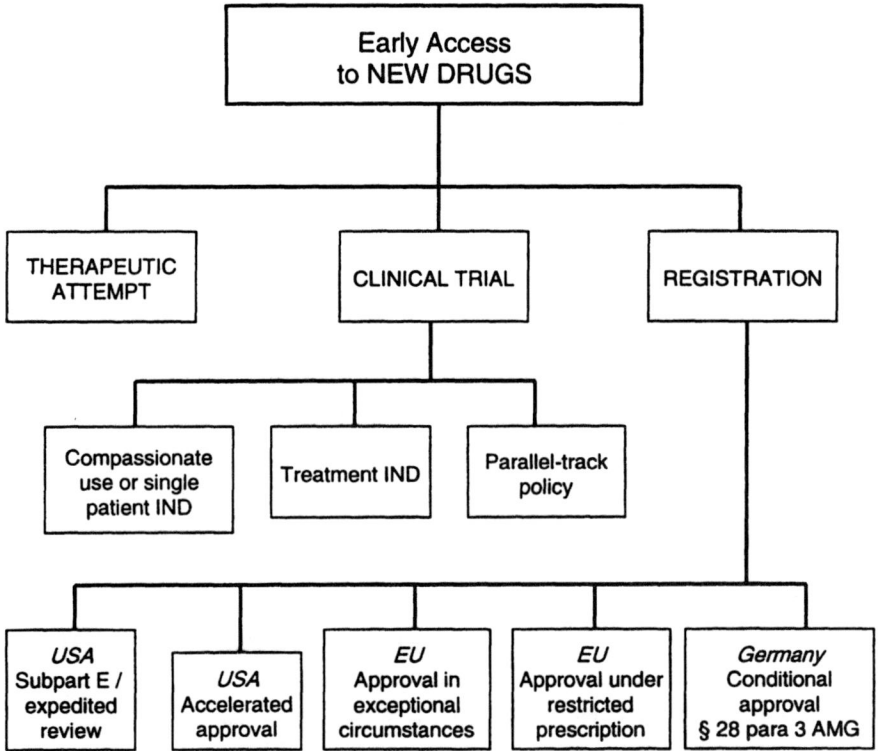

Figure 6.1 Early access to new drugs

made available to patients outside the more traditional drug development format.

Treatment IND

The treatment IND is a regulation which allows access to drugs which studies have shown are possibly effective in treating desperately ill patients, while pharmaceutical manufacturers continue to pursue marketing authorisation. The regulation was *"intended to facilitate the availability of promising new drugs as early in the drug development process as possible .... to patients with serious and life-threatening diseases for which no comparable or satisfactory alternative drug or other therapies exist"*.

FDA regulations formally recognise the treatment IND, allowing its use in cases in which:

(a) there is sufficient evidence of safety and efficacy;
(b) the potential benefits outweigh the risks; and
(c) the medical condition under study is a serious disease with no satisfactory therapies.

Parallel-track policy

A policy statement issued in 1992 allows for the expanded availability of investigational drugs through a "parallel-track" mechanism under which promising new drugs for treating AIDS and other HIV-related diseases can be made available as early as possible for patients who have no alternative treatments. This policy makes drugs available to patients who cannot enter Phase III clinical trials while these are in progress. This programme is testimony to the direct involvement of advocacy groups, especially those representing people with AIDS. Unlike the treatment IND, the parallel-track approach allows expanded availability based almost exclusively on safety data, that means at the end of Phase I.

Accelerated approval and Subpart E procedures

The aforementioned approaches must be distinguished from possible ways of expediting the development and approval of new drugs, such as Subpart E procedures and accelerated approval.

The accelerated approval regulation (21 CFR 314.500), which appeared in the Federal Register on 1 December 1992 (FR Vol 57, No 239, pp. 58942–58960) allows the FDA to approve new drugs or biologicals intended for treatment of serious illnesses and that offer meaningful therapeutic benefits compared with existing treatment based on surrogate marker results, while clinical trials continue to determine if clinical endpoints confirm earlier results.

In contrast, the Subpart E procedures are designed to accelerate the development of new therapies. One important element of this rule is close consultation with the FDA. The FDA assists sponsors in designing adequate trials to evaluate the safety and efficacy of the drug. There are two types of FDA–sponsor consultations:

(a) Pre-Investigational New Drug (IND) Meetings
    Prior to an IND submission, the sponsor may request a meeting "to review and reach agreement on the design of animal studies needed to initiate human testing."
(b) End-of-Phase I Meetings
    After Phase I data are available, the sponsor may again request a meeting to "review and reach agreement on the design of Phase II controlled clinical trials, with the goal that such testing will be adequate to provide sufficient data on the drug's safety and effectiveness to support a decision on its approvability for marketing".

EU

Council regulation (EEC, no 2309/93) (EEC, 1993) states that in the EU the company may submit an application through the centralised procedure (Figure 6.2) under "exceptional circumstances" (Part 4 G to the Annex to Directive 75/318 EEC) (EEC, 1995) which are that:

(a) the indications are extremely rare; or
(b) the state of scientific knowledge is not advanced enough; or
(c) tests are forbidden on grounds of medical ethics.

In these circumstances marketing authorisation may be granted under the following conditions:

(a) the applicant completes an identified programme of studies within a time period specified by the competent authority, the results of which shall form the basis of a reassessment of the benefit/risk profile;
(b) the medicinal product in question may be supplied on medical prescription only and may in certain cases be administered only under strict medical supervision, possibly in a hospital, and for a radiopharmaceutical by an authorised person;

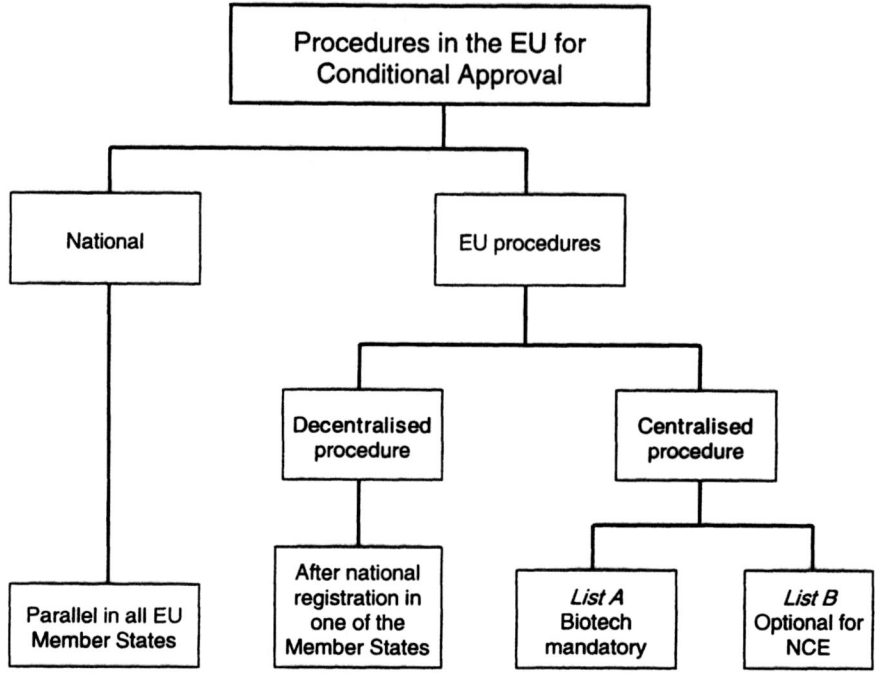

Figure 6.2 Procedures in the EU for conditional approval

(c)   the package leaflet and any medical information shall draw the attention of the medical practitioner to the fact that the particulars available concerning the medicinal product in question are as yet inadequate in certain specified respects.

Besides this, there is the possibility within the centralised procedure of the EU that a medicinal product may be authorised under the conditions of restricted prescription (92/26/EEC:Article 3) (EEC, 1992). These are: exclusive treatment in a hospital environment, diagnosis in specialised diagnostic institutions and prescription only by specialist and specialist supervision through treatment because of very serious side-effects.

Companies may request scientific advice during development, similar to a pre-IND meeting in the USA.

Conditional approval in Germany

Contrary to the USA, a "therapeutic attempt" (Therapieversuch), i.e. the use of a not yet approved medicinal product in a single patient or in a small number of patients, is not considered by the relevant legislation in Germany (German Drug Law, *AMG*). The physician performing a "therapeutic attempt" is solely liable and the trial is subject to criminal law (34 StGB).

In Germany a physician assumes a very special degree of responsibility if he decides to use a drug for an unorthodox or non-approved indication or if he uses an unauthorised drug; in such cases, if injury results and an action is brought against him, he must be able to show that his decision to adopt this course was well-founded and in the patient's apparent interest, and that the patient was informed as to any known risks.

The German Drug Law allows the granting of a "provisional" authorisation, according to § 28 paragraph 3 German Drug Law (Figure 6.3). In such a case authorisation is connected with the condition that the applicant submits certain test results "by a specified time after authorisation has been granted...". This procedure is applied when it is in the public interest to have a certain product immediately introduced onto the market because of its high therapeutic value though further essential data are still needed for a comprehensive product assessment.

Requirements for approvals

The conditions under which postponement of some of the tests is possible, as defined in § 28 para 3 AMG, are that there is sufficient evidence that the product has a great therapeutic value and therefore it is in the public interest to have the product immediately placed on the market.

"Sufficient evidence" means that plausible and clear evidence of efficacy is available (e.g. a surrogate/or secondary endpoint is measured and correlation between the surrogate parameter and the definitive "true" endpoint is well supported by indirect efficacy endpoints). The following situations are not acceptable:

Conditional Approval   § 28 para 3 AMG

Furthermore, the competent federal higher authority may impose conditions prescribing additional analytic and pharmacological–toxicological tests or clinical trials to be carried out and a report submitted on the results, if the drug has a high therapeutic value and if, therefore, it is in the public interest to have the drug immediately introduced onto the market, yet if additional essential details are still required to enable a comprehensive assessment of the drug

---

Figure 6.3 Legal basis for conditional approval – German Drug Law

(a)   the mere claim or presumption of such benefits;
(b)   evidence of non-essential parameters (or such that cannot be extrapolated) or of methodologically controversial parameters.

"Great therapeutic value" means, in the given legal context, that considerable clinically relevant therapeutic benefits are expected, such as:

(a)   treatment in a new indication with a strong need of treatment (offering new therapeutic fields);
(b)   considerable therapeutic advancement in known indication;
(c)   clear advantage over therapeutic alternatives (improved efficacy, improved safety profile).

A "public interest" can be assumed when the product will considerably improve the likelihood of a medical cure; only then can the disadvantages connected with the procedure of granting conditional approval (i.e. incomplete testing) be justified.

In Germany there is also the possibility of applying for priority processing (i.e. same concept as "fast-track" approval). The priority processing of applications is admissible on condition that a cursory review (on the basis of a medical pre-review referring to the expert reports) shows that the product may qualify for approval under § 28 para 3 AMG. The prerequisites for this procedure are:

1. Presentation of considerable clinically relevant therapeutic benefits; and
2. Sufficient plausibility and, as a minimum, documentary evidence of efficacy and safety.

If it is evident after a cursory review that an application has no chance of successfully qualifying for preferred processing, (e.g. because there is no plausible proof of efficacy or because of obviously unacceptable risks), then it is rejected for this procedure even if it claims important indications.

Procedure

The pharmaceutical company applies explicitly for a § 28 para 3 AMG and justifies the great therapeutic value of the medicinal product. Immediately after submission of such an application, as a rule within a few weeks, the applicant is informed about the outcome of the assessment by the so-called *clearing unit* of the institute. If the application is not accepted, reasons for the rejection are given.

The following criteria are routinely checked in assessing the claim of a great therapeutic value of a new substance or a new indication of a known substance:

(a) Lack of Therapeutic Alternatives
Great therapeutic value appears evident and the risks are judged to be justifiable, on the basis of a review of the expert opinion and a random sample check of the documented data justifying the claim. The primary endpoints investigated in clinical trials must be such that therapeutic efficacy can be extrapolated from them. The documents submitted must allow intersubject review of the results. The trials must have used the medicinal product of the application; in cases where results have been obtained with another product then it must be demonstrated that the results are transferable.

(b) Better Benefit/Risk Ratio than in any Therapeutic Alternative

(c) Risk-Reducing Route of Administration
A new route of administration has been developed where the risks are reduced and the therapeutic efficacy not changed.

The German Bundesinstitut für Arzneimittel und Medizinprodukte (BfArM, Federal Institute for Drugs and Medical Devices) does not always meet the requests of applicants for a § 28 para 3 AMG procedure, since this approach takes much of the institute's capacity. Some pharmaceutical companies seem to request this procedure for any of their applications just to enjoy faster processing of their applications. Of the 68 conditional approvals granted under § 28 AMG in the past year, only one was for a new chemical entity (NCE).

Issues concerning conditional licensing

Ethical aspects

Medical ethics is traditionally understood as the commitment of medical professionals to the physical and mental health of their patients. However, the unshakeable, unalterable and definitive classic ethical principles of causing no hazard to patients, of self-determination, of justice, of social benefit, more often than not may clash in everyday medical routine, plunging doctors into situations of conflict. We are facing a worldwide trend to shift the responsibility for decision-taking in medicine from the individual doctor to institutions such as ethics committees.

Technological development, but also general socio-political changes, have started to impact on medical ethics to the effect that the classic Hippocratic principles are to be extended or otherwise modified. Also economic and competitive pressures will, or have already started to, exert their influences on medical ethics, so that other than purely patient-oriented motives may influence doctors' decisions on therapies and research.

Medical ethics change as society changes. It must be accepted that there will be variations in the approach to certain aspects of ethics. These variations in approach may be related to cultural or national differences to the social environment or even to political persuasions.

Media and pressure groups

The news about a new therapy in life-threatening diseases is disseminated rapidly by the active media, be it by radio, television or the press. The industry must avoid misleading reports in the early stages of clinical trials. Press coverage in favour of the use of such drugs may raise false hopes and expectations, e.g. in cancer patients and patients with multiple sclerosis. Pressure groups of the patients concerned may try to enforce an accelerated approval of the drug on the basis of preliminary information.

Clinical evaluation of efficacy and safety

Substances to be used for serious illnesses, e.g. in oncology and in the treatment of AIDS, are by their very nature in an exceptional situation with regard to pre-registration requirements. On the basis of their possible life-saving properties there is general agreement that the drugs should be brought into human use at a much earlier stage than other drugs, even when only limited safety and efficacy information is available. As a consequence, regulatory authorities in several countries have developed special procedures to allow early entrance into clinical studies.

Control agencies may often feel pressurised to release drugs for life-threatening diseases at a time when the knowledge of the effect of the drug is very limited, before full documentation is available. Efficacy is often only supported by invalidated, questionable surrogate parameters. In a recent publication, Robert Temple described this very accurately: "We have, on the one hand, growing impatience with our inability to find treatments for serious illnesses – multiple sclerosis, amyotrophic lateral sclerosis, Alzheimer's disease, most solid tumours, AIDS and AIDS-opportunistic infections. There is a strong sense of "hurry-up". All of this drives us towards utilising the

63

earliest, most readily determined evidence of effectiveness, generally evidence of an effect on surrogate or "intermediate" endpoints.

On the other hand, there are forces urging us towards measuring the ultimate clinical endpoints: survival, disability, capacity for functioning in daily life. These forces are:

- Disappointment in the results of using either surrogate or intermediate endpoints, including some major surprises.

- Recent success in measuring small but very valuable real effects, using larger trials and meta-analyses. These successes are most conspicuous in the cardiovascular area but have also occurred in other settings, such as adjuvant chemotherapy for breast and colon cancer.

- Growing concern with the financial cost of therapy in relation to benefits and increasing interest in the true clinical value of intervention.

In the middle of all this are the regulatory agencies, trying hard to get the balance right." (Temple, 1995). The identification of surrogate markers with regard to acceptance as well supported substitutes for the real efficacy endpoints should have absolute priority.

After granting early access to drugs for life-threatening diseases, clinical testing for efficacy and safety must be completed through post-approval (Phase IV) studies. Regulatory authorities must develop ways of ensuring that the conditions of conditional licences are satisfied. As yet there is little experience in this area.

Discussion

The provisional authorisation of medicinal products for life-threatening diseases is largely advocated by most parties involved. There is much political and social pressure from interested groups in many countries trying to influence political forces towards the early approval of these drugs. This has been quite successful, especially in the USA.

There are, however, critical voices from the regulatory and scientific community warning against the early use of drugs that have not been sufficiently tested for safety and efficacy, for ethical and scientific reasons (Liebenau, 1990). They say that accelerated drug approvals will yield far more benefits to the pharmaceutical industry than to the public and would permit the widespread sale and supply of unproved and possibly ineffective new products. To remove the doubt, criticism and fear, there is a need to discuss with all parties involved in rational drug therapy the levels of proof of efficacy and safety of drugs for life-threatening diseases required under the special conditions of a conditional approval. Especially with regard to efficacy, an intensive discussion about the validation of surrogate markers is much needed.

References

EEC (1975). Council Directive 75/318/EEC of 20 May 1975 on the approximation of the laws of Member States relating to analytical, pharmacotoxicological and clinical standards and protocols in respect of the testing of proprietary medicinal products (OJ No L 147 of 9.6.1975), Annex Part 4 G.

EEC (1992). Council Directive 92/26/EEC of 31 March 1992 concerning the classification for the supply of medicinal products for human use (OJ No L 113 of 30.4.1992), Article 3 No 3.

EEC (1993). Council Regulation No (EEC) 2309/93 of 22 July 1993 laying down Community procedures for the authorisation and supervision of medicinal products for human and veterinary use and establishing a European Agency for the Evaluation of Medicinal Products (OJ No L 214 of 24.8.1993).

Liebenau J (1990). The rise of the British pharmaceutical industry. *British Medical Journal*, **301**: 724–8, 733.

Mathieu M (1990). *Drug Accessibility Programs for the Desperately Ill, Newly Revised and Updated.* PAREXEL International Corporation, Cambridge, MA, Chapter 21, pp. 257–274.

Nightingale S (1994). Procedures for registration of drugs for AIDS and other life-threatening diseases. In *Seventh International Conference of Drug Regulatory Authorities. The Hague, Netherlands 18–22 April 1994*, WHO/DMP/CDRA/94.1, 38–42.

Temple RJ (1995). A regulatory authority's opinion about surrogate endpoints. In Nimmo WS and Tucker GT (eds) *Clinical Measurement in Drug Evaluation*, John Wiley & Sons Ltd.

7 Dialogue and interaction between regulators and sponsors: Formal, informal or none at all?

DANN M MICHOLS

Summary

1. A two-year programme of re-engineering in the Canadian Drugs Directorate is essentially complete. It recognises industry as a partner, and client, with whom full and open communications are a necessity.

2. A number of opportunities for interaction have been implemented, including pre-Investigational New Drug (IND) meetings, pre-New Drug Submission (NDS) meetings and post-Notice of Non-compliance (NON) meetings; industry liaison committee meetings, information sessions and the like. Dialogue is essential to the Directorate's way of doing business; however industry must recognise that it is a two-way process.

3. Formal mechanisms of dialogue and interaction offer a number of benefits compared to informal contact. They tend to be more successful, more productive and they ensure consistency and fairness for all concerned.

4.   A Management of Drug Submissions Policy lays out the expectations and requirements of the regulator and the rights and privileges of the manufacturer. There are two opportunities for appeal. Although management of the review process has become more Draconian in Canada, in exchange performance targets for the Directorate's review processes have been set and performance has been greatly enhanced.

5.   Ensuring that dialogue and interaction remains timely and effective will be a challenging responsibility for both the regulator and the industry.

Introduction

The Canadian Drugs Directorate (the Directorate) is just concluding an intense two-year programme of re-engineering, called "Drugs Directorate Renewal". Under this renewal, there were few major issues facing the Drugs Directorate that were not addressed; some 60 major issues in all, encompassing mandate, policy, process, organisation, automation, resources, and systems.

Although the Renewal process is officially coming to a close, it cannot be the end of renewal. As with all good quality improvement initiatives, there is a need to go deeper in some areas and to solidify the positive gains made in others. For several reasons, the drug review process will be examined in considerably more detail. One outcome of the Drugs Directorate Renewal is a Vision Statement which says, *inter alia*: "We will endeavour to provide national and international leadership in drug regulation from a foundation of intelligent programming, constructive partnerships, full and open communications, and a productive organizational culture".

How can full and open communication with industry, one of the principal partners, be achieved? A survey of the Directorate's staff revealed that there are considerable differences of opinion concerning the amount of dialogue and interaction that should take place between regulators and sponsors and the stage at which it is appropriate.

This paper discusses the value of dialogue and whether it should be formal or informal, from the viewpoint of the Canadian Drugs Directorate; the proposition of no dialogue at all is untenable these days.

The value of dialogue

The Drugs Directorate is finalising its Strategic Framework, a document designed by management, but consulted upon by all staff, to explain what is important to the Directorate and how it will make decisions. This guide states explicitly that the Directorate is open to any and all interventions that might ensure that it understands fully the pressures on, and ambitions of, product sponsors **and** that might convey an understanding of the realities and pressures we, as regulators, face.

In other words, dialogue and interaction are seen as essential to the Directorate's business, but it is a two-way street. This concept is not well understood by some sectors of Canadian industry. Regulators work within a context just as industry does; truly successful dialogue will be based on a mutual understanding of those realities.

Regulators must act within the constraints of legislation and regulations, limited resources and various interpretations of the public good. However, since industry is viewed as a partner, and as a client in Canada, industry collectively must be fully consulted on the development of processes, procedures, and instruments of review in the broad sense, and sponsors individually must be given full opportunity to present their cases in the narrower sense of the submission review function.

To this end, a number of initiatives have been implemented, including opportunities for meetings, development of guidelines, and production of discussion papers or policy documents. Expert Advisory Committee meetings, and regular industry liaison committee meetings, have been instituted. In the introduction of cost recovery or fees for service, information sessions, issue seminars, and resolution workshops, have been held. All of this activity is very resource-intensive but dialogue with industry is absolutely essential.

The value of the dialogue should be given with one caveat. Industry is not the only stakeholder. In Canada, equal time and opportunity for input must be given to provincial governments, private sector drug plans, the health professions, researchers, consumers, and the general public. A successful regulatory regime requires not a dialogue, but a "multilogue".

Formal or informal?

From personal experience, the more successful mechanisms and instruments of consultation seem to have two things in common – formality and commonality. The more defined and planned the exercise, the more successful. The more time spent defining and understanding the problems or concerns of both parties, the more productive.

Formal mechanisms of dialogue and interaction ensure consistency. They ensure that a process has been developed, communicated, and represents the institution. A process which is institutional has a better chance of not being arbitrary and therefore should ensure fairness to the individual submission sponsor, to all submission sponsors, to the individual reviewer, and to all reviewers.

During the actual process of the review of a submission, there should be limited, or no **informal,** contact between reviewers and manufacturers – for the protection of both reviewer and sponsor. As a consequence, in Canada we have tried to ensure the institutionalisation of the review.

Re-development of the review process

Improving the regulatory review process does not only mean speeding it up. In Canada, we are trying to promote a delicate balance between healthcare objectives and industrial development objectives. The Canadian Drugs Directorate is committed to addressing the issue of enhanced performance, defined as a function of the quality of a submission, the efficiency of the review process, and the resources that can be applied to that process. All three variables must be addressed.

In its initial re-development of review processes, the Directorate developed and published (and upgraded twice) a Management of Drug Submissions Policy. This lays out the expectations and requirements of the regulator, and the rights and privileges of the manufacturer. There are a number of points for interaction.

1. A submission is first screened against published guidelines. If there are deficiencies, a notice of screening deficiency is issued and the submission rejected. This decision is appealable and there is a performance target for the process.
2. If a submission is accepted for review and subsequently a minor deficiency is found, a clarifax is issued. The sponsor has 10 days

to respond with the missing information. If a serious deficiency is found, or if the submission is found not to be in compliance with the Food and Drug Act, a Notice of Deficiency (NOD) or a Notice of Non-Compliance (NON) is issued. The sponsor has 90 days to respond or convince the Bureau Director that there is good reason to extend the period. This decision is appealable.

3. If the sponsor responds with the relevant information, the review continues. If the submission is still found to be lacking, a NON-withdrawal letter is issued and the file is closed. This decision too is appealable.

Management of the review process has, by necessity, become more Draconian. In exchange, performance targets have been fixed for all of the Directorate's review processes and a two-tiered appeal process put in place. Although outside experts are not used on committees in the decision process, they will be used in the appeal process.

There is an obligation to clearly communicate guidelines for all review processes, to ensure the sponsors understand what is required. In recognition of this, the Directorate has heavily invested resources into this communications process, and consulted with all stakeholders on the contents of all guidelines.

Electronic templates

Electronic templates have been developed for both the Chemistry and Manufacturing (C&M) assessment process and the Clinical/Preclinical Evaluation process. The C&M template, completed by the sponsor, forms the comprehensive summary for review. The clinical template for the moment is an internal review tool but a pilot version is already being tested with several sponsors. By following these templates, it is difficult for the sponsor to format or complete the submission incorrectly. All guidelines and templates are either on the Directorate's electronic bulletin board or soon will be. They can be down-loaded and submitted electronically.

Types of meetings

A number of opportunities for sponsors to meet with reviewers and their research support have been built into the Canadian review processes. These include pre-IND (Investigational New Drug) meetings to discuss and approve broad plans for clinical trials, and pre-NDS (New Drug Submission) meetings for sponsors to discuss the information required in a submission and the approach to take. There can also be post-NON meetings if a sponsor wishes to understand better the deficiencies of its submission after review.

The important point here is that all of these meetings are "institutional", in that there are ground-rules for them set by the organisation rather than by an individual reviewer or bureau. The meetings are off-line from the review process so that the performance standards set for review cover only activities over which a reviewer has control.

Performance standards have now been set for all steps of the review process. While they exist to enable reviewers and management to track performance and make corrections, their very existence adds a formality to the process.

Tracking

An electronic Drug Submission Tracking System has been put into place to track performance. The status of all submissions can be determined at any point. Despite the fact that the Directorate publishes performance targets so that sponsors should be able to calculate where in the process their submissions are, reviewers are constantly inundated with calls for status reports. Recently, the technology was put into place to enable each sponsor to access the status of its, and only its, submissions electronically. Now that this is in place, another informal interaction has been eliminated.

Appeal mechanisms

As processes become more Draconian and as performance standards become more rigorous, there is an increasing need for appeal mechanisms which are fair to all parties. As well, appeals must be dealt with in a timely fashion. There are provisions for financial penalties if the Directorate does not meet its performance targets on a submission. Just as a sponsor does not want its submission thrown out arbitrarily because a reviewer is behind schedule, so too the Directorate does not want inadequate files slowing down the reviewers. A fair appeal system is essential but again the existence of an exacting appeal process adds another level of formality to the interactions between agency and sponsor.

Conclusion

In conclusion, dialogue and interaction take time and money. They are essential but as industry puts more and more pressure on the regulator for "timely review", the mechanisms used for interaction will become more formal, more institutional, and more "generic" (i.e. not unique to an individual sponsor).

Interaction mechanisms will be built into the review and compliance processes so that they can be time-controlled or they will be taken off-line from the process of reviewing a particular submission. They will become more electronic to consume less real time in getting information to the reviewer by using E-mail and fax rather than the telephone.

With all these limitations and conditions, making sure that dialogue and interaction remains timely and effective will be a challenging responsibility for both the regulator and the industry.

8 The use of electronic dossiers or CANDAs: Help or hindrance?

ROGER WILLIAMS and DAVID ISOM

Summary

1. Computer-assisted NDAs (CANDAs) have been used for the past 10 years; and in general the response of reviewers to CANDAs has been positive. Both the degree and the quality of interaction with sponsors have improved, and a comparison of non-CANDA and CANDA submissions suggests that electronic submission may help to reduce review times.

2. The recent SMART (submission management and review tracking) initiative of the Food and Drug Administration (FDA) (the Agency) is designed to expedite the review process for both new drugs and new biologics through the development of automated systems. SMART projects are underway at the Agency level, as well as at the level of the Center for Drug Evaluation and Research (CDER) and the Center for Biologics Evaluation and Research (CBER). The Agency-level projects include the establishment of electronic data interchange standards with sponsors (ICH M2), and the harmonisation of computer systems Agency-wide. CDER's projects include: (1) the computer assisted review of safety (CARS), (2) archiving; and (3) administrative management of the files (AMF).

3. Substantial progress has already been made in the field of CANDAs, and for electronic submissions in general. However, a number of issues remain, particularly access to data and depth of review, databases and confidentiality, and harmonisation.

Experience with CANDAs

Computer-assisted NDAs (CANDAs), which were introduced by the Center for Drug Evaluation and Research (CDER) in 1985, largely on an experimental basis, have become more elaborate and refined over the years. The Center has undertaken two assessments of CANDA submissions; the first applied to 23 submissions during 1985–88 and the second to 63 submissions during 1988–92. Detailed results of these assessments were published in 1994 (US Department of Health and Human Services, 1994).

Each of the ten review divisions within CDER gained some experience with CANDAs; the anti-infectives division received the most electronic submissions during 1988–92 (Figure 8.1). The annual number of CANDAs received did not follow any particular pattern; the development of many (45%) had been contracted out by the sponsor to a third party. In order to improve the understanding of CANDA utility and effectiveness, CDER review staff were interviewed for their opinions about CANDAs. In general, these opinions were positive; certainly the degree and the quality of interaction with sponsors were improved (in 67% and 65% of cases, respectively) when CANDAs were employed. Rapid access to information was acknowledged as a valuable aspect of CANDAs by the majority of reviewers (Figure 8.2). However, a critical question is how the average approval times for CANDA submissions compare to paper NDAs.

A comparison of non-CANDA and CANDA submissions that were provided to the FDA in a fixed period of time suggests that CANDAs reduced the review time during 1993–94 by 14 months (Figure 8.3). Although there may be some selection bias or other confounding factors, such as the length of the dossier (shorter documents lend themselves to the electronic format) or the number of applications reviewed, these data suggest that well-designed CANDAs can reduce drug approval times.

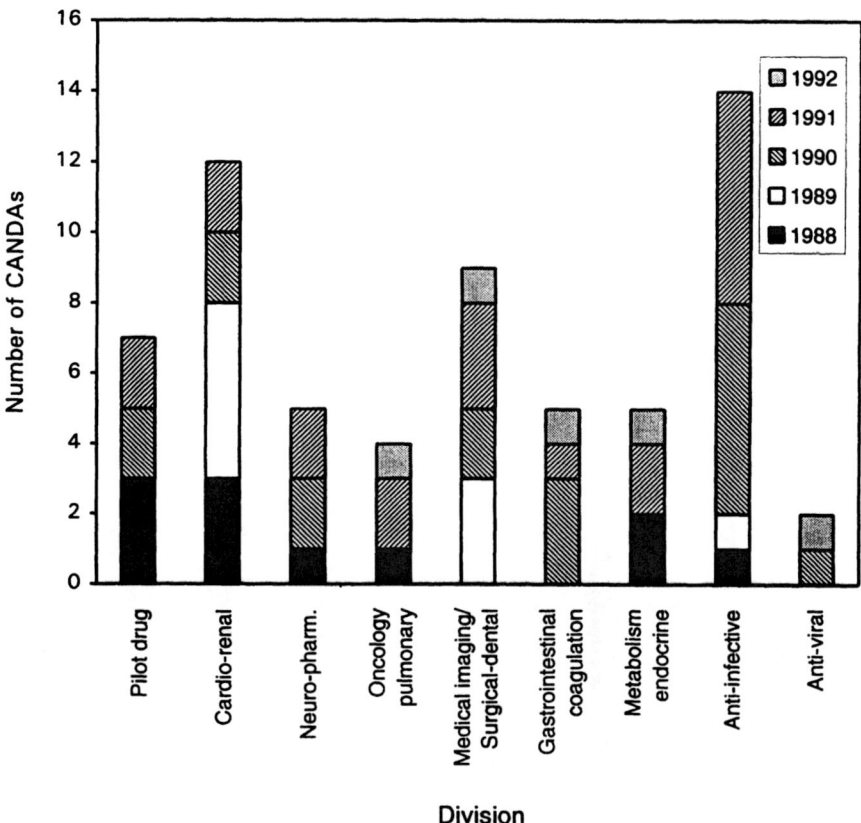

Figure 8.1 CANDAs by CDER division (1988–1992)

The SMART initiative

There is no exact definition of a CANDA; it can vary from being simply an electronic way of reading the submission to providing information in a random access database. In addition, different companies have used different computer systems and varying practices have been adopted by the different review divisions within CDER. The next evolutionary step was to evaluate the development of information management systems, through the SMART initiative.

The purpose of SMART is to expedite the review process for new drugs and biologics through the development of automated systems to support the review process and the management of electronic

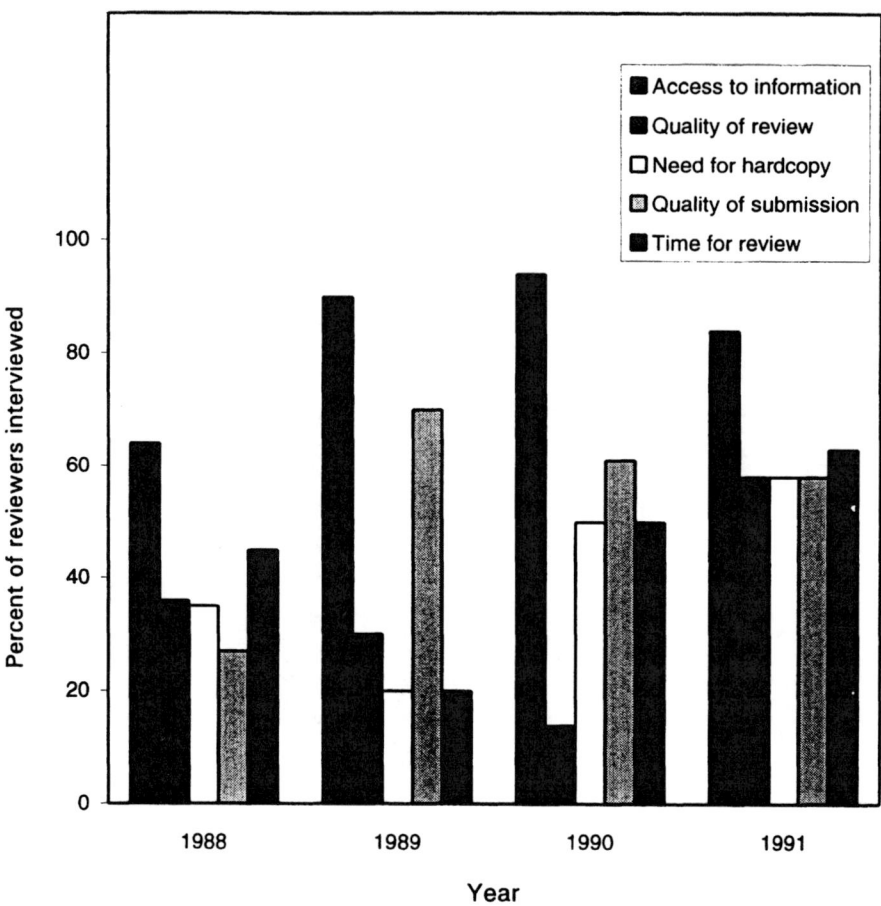

Figure 8.2 Opinions of FDA reviewers on valuable aspects of CANDAs

submissions and the documents thus generated. The aim is to work with sponsors to establish data interchange standards to support electronic submissions and to harmonise, where possible, the computer systems being developed throughout the Agency.

A number of projects are included under the SMART initiative; some of these are discussed in the following sections.

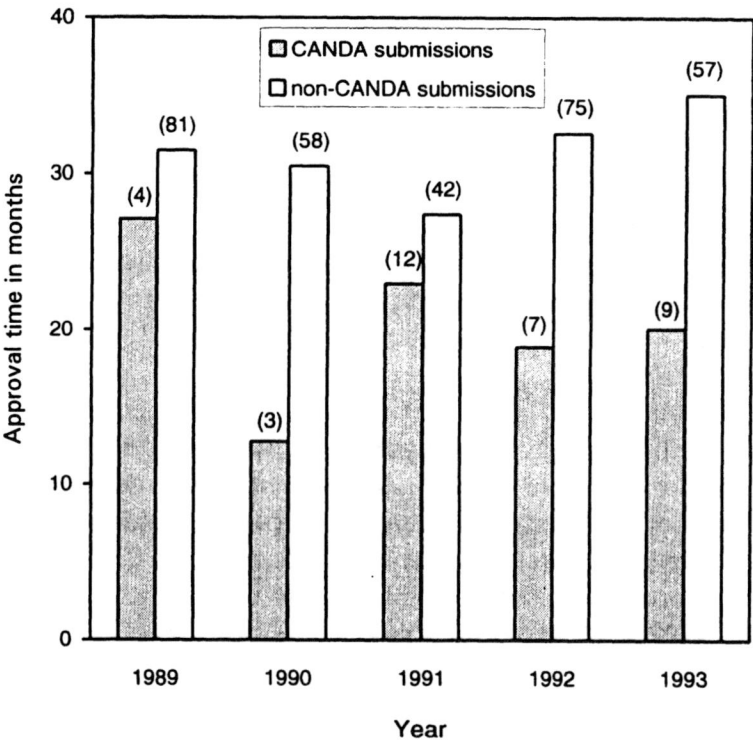

Figure 8.3 Comparison of average approval time for electronic and paper-based submisssions

Safety review

The computer-assisted review of safety (CARS), also known as the integrated safety summary (ISS), is a CDER IT initiative to provide automated, standardised tools that increase the consistency of NDA safety data analyses, with the ability to support customised analyses. It will be a large database utilising commercial, off-the-shelf software and should be compatible with certain other projects. CARS may provide a powerful tool to quickly scan large amounts of information and readily identify abnormalities.

Archiving

The archiving project is focused on establishing archiving standards for electronic submissions. It is one of the CDER projects under the SMART initiative which presents a particular challenge in relation to electronic submissions. Technology is advancing so rapidly that the ability to read electronic dossiers can soon be lost, e.g. new word-processing programmes may not access old files. The Agency will continue to store paper copies until this problem can be solved.

Administrative management of the files (AMF)

CDER's administrative management of the files (AMF) project focused on how document management technologies can improve the way review staff archive, manage, search, and retrieve electronic submissions and internally generated documents. The goal of the project is a desktop database interface to the CDER local area network (LAN), that provides access to review-related document repositories and workflow management tools.

International Conference on Harmonisation (ICH)

The Agency's ICH M2 expert working group is making substantial progress on the challenge of developing electronic standards for the transfer of information and data. A data transport mechanism is needed to provide the link, or pipeline, through which data crosses the data transport interface between sponsor and regulatory agency; a pilot demonstration was presented at the ICH3 conference in Yokohoma (November 1995). The obstacles to be overcome include transmission standards, security, confidentiality and integrity of the data.

The future

Substantial progress has already been made concerning the receipt of electronic data from industry into CDER to facilitate the assessment process. Rather than focusing on review division and drug

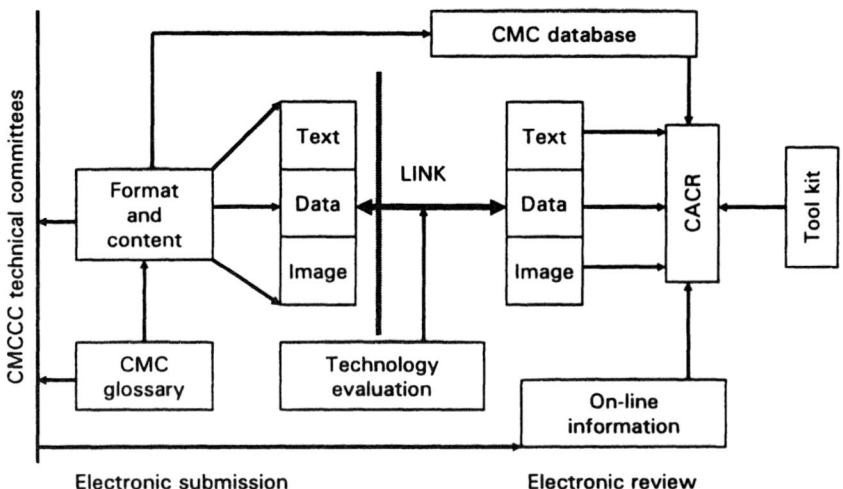

Figure 8.4 Flow of chemistry, manufacturing and controls (CMC) data
CMCCC, Chemistry, Manufacturing and Controls Co-ordinating Committee;
CACR, Computer-Assisted Chemistry Review

class, we might focus on the subject topics in a dossier, i.e. (i)
clinical/statistical; (ii) pharmacology/toxicology; (iii) chemistry,
manufacturing and controls; (iv) clinical pharmacology; (v) biopharmaceutics and (vi) microbiology. Text, data and images which have
been structured through format and content decisions could flow
into the Agency through an "ICH-type" link (Figure 8.4); it would
then be redistributed into the Agency's platforms where reviewers
by discipline could accept the information to produce a review. As
industry is already creating electronic files the challenge is not
insurmountable; with the will, resources and interest it could
happen over the next 5–10 years.

Conclusions

In the field of electronic submissions, a number of issues remain for
which solutions are being sought. In the face of a truly automatic
submission, could access to data ever be limited? How can the

confidentiality of databases be maintained and can true harmonisation be achieved? How can the assessment proceed without unnecessary "data dredging?" These are just a few of the challenges we currently face.

Reference

CANDA Guidance Manual 2nd Edition, October 1994. Washington DC: US Department of Health and Human Services, Public Health Service, Food and Drug Administration.

9 The exchange of assessment reports and training of assessors

ANDRE BROEKMANS

Summary

1. The ideal assessors should be open for peer review, in active interaction with colleagues of other authorities, involved in continuing education and active in regulatory research. The training of assessors generally occurs in-house, the master–apprentice relationship being supplemented with academic courses and attendance at conferences.

2. Both the training of assessors and the exchange of assessment reports will enhance the review process. A prerequisite for the exchange of assessment reports is a harmonised structure and content for the dossier. The assessment report will be one of the cornerstones of the new regulatory system within Europe.

3. Experience gained through the Pharmaceutical Evaluation Report (PER) Scheme indicates that the exchange of assessment reports can provide assurance, a second opinion and useful perspective on outstanding problems. In the future it may provide a substitute for national review. However, there is no evidence that it necessarily expedites the review process.

Introduction

There is no doubt that both the exchange of assessment reports and the training of assessors will improve the regulatory review process. This paper focuses on these two topics, drawing on the experience within Europe and with the Pharmaceutical Evaluation Report (PER) Scheme. The PER Scheme is approaching the transnational ideal, as several non-European countries participate with those from Europe:

> From EFTA*: Austria, Finland, Iceland, Norway, Sweden, Switzerland;
>
> From the EU: Germany, Ireland, Italy, the Netherlands, the United Kingdom;
>
> Others: Australia, Canada, Hungary, South Africa, New Zealand.

*European Free Trade Association

It allows not only the exchange of reports but also provides education opportunities for assessors.

Training of assessors

The training of assessors is always regarded as an in-house responsibility. Most authorities use the master–apprentice relationship as an important tool. In addition, in-house courses are offered and the junior assessor is allowed to attend academic courses, workshops and conferences. For a medical assessor, for example, the core of the education programme may consist of pharmacokinetics, clinical epidemiology and medical statistics. However, among authorities the prerequisites of a qualified assessor in terms of knowledge, skills and attitudes are seldom the subject of discussion.

Anyone wishing to become an assessor will probably have a scientific education and good writing skills, preferably in English. In addition, each assessor must have specialist knowledge relevant to the dossier, yet be able to assess the general parts of the dossier as well. Importantly, all assessors should be independent; in the European system assessors have to declare their interests.

Probably of more importance is the notion that assessors should remain in active interaction with the scientific community and not become an isolated desk-assessor. The Medicines Evaluation Board in the Netherlands stipulates that assessors will have other responsibilities as well, be it in the laboratory or in a university hospital. In addition, authorities should create the conditions for continuing education to develop knowledge and skills. Assessors should actively participate in scientific conferences and keep track of the latest developments.

The ideal assessor

The ideal assessor would be open to peer review so that the regulatory review process might be continuously improved. In the Netherlands, reports prepared by assessors are discussed by the Board and feedback is provided on the quality of the report; there is no formal system for criticism by colleagues. To better understand and solve differences in the assessment of the same medicinal product, assessors should ideally be in active interaction with colleagues from other regulatory authorities. This readily occurs within Europe where collaborative workshops and training programmes allow colleagues to meet and discuss relevant topics. However, it is my experience, with the former concertation procedure and the current centralised procedure within Europe, that assessors from different authorities often reach the same scientific conclusion. This is one of the reasons why the Netherlands' Medicines Evaluation Board refrains from assessing the pharmaceutical part of the dossier of a synthetic drug when the product has been approved in one of the Member States within the previous 5 years.

The European Union (EU) provides opportunities for continuing education within the field of regulatory medicine through special meetings, often organised at the initiative of one of the Member States. These meetings concentrate on specific topics with a regulatory perspective. In addition, within the PER Scheme, a tradition has built up for seminars, not only to contribute to the personal develop-ment of the assessor, but also to enhance understanding and collabo-ration in the review of medicines. Harmonisation of the assessment can be further enhanced through the exchange of assessors; in the Netherlands exchanges have occurred with Spain, Denmark and Sweden.

An important objective for ideal assessors is active participation in regulatory research. Experience shows that this can be difficult as information provided by industry must be regarded as confidential. In the Netherlands we are fortunate in having reached a consensus with our national industry on how to proceed with publications based on dossiers. Now we are able to share some of our regulatory activities with the scientific community.

In many ways the assessor is an anonymous scientist; few are aware of the job and it goes unrewarded. It can be difficult to pursue that kind of career, although compensation comes from being in-volved in the intriguing hand-over from science to practice. For any regulatory authority, the challenge is to keep a critical mass of high quality scientists to carry out assessments.

Exchange of assessment reports

A prerequisite for the exchange of assessment reports is to have a harmonised structure for the dossier. This approach already facili-tates exchange within the European Union and between a number of non-EU countries. At the very least there must be an identical data-base, and, especially within European Member States, a goal to reach a common Summary of Product Characteristics (SmPC). This is one of the aims of the International Conference on Harmonisation (ICH) which, in the end, will contribute to the global harmonisation of dossiers. The structure and content of the assessment report must also be agreed before exchange can take place. In Europe this has a long history which started with the initiative to establish the voluntary PER Scheme. The guideline on assessment reports, used for many years within the PER Scheme, and subsequently integrated into the

European system, was the basis for the new guideline agreed by the Committee for Proprietary Medicinal Products (CPMP) in 1994.

The European assessment report

Under the current guidelines, the assessment report will become the cornerstone for the new regulatory procedures within Europe. Within the mutual recognition procedure it should enable the Member States to recognise the assessment of the Reference Member State. In the centralised procedure the assessment report of the rapporteur and co-rapporteur, together with the expert reports, will be the only documentation available to members of the CPMP.

There are two important aspects to the new European guidelines which should facilitate quality assurance of the whole regulatory process. First, the assessment report should make reference to the dossier, by indicating the kind of data on which the assessor's deliberations and conclusions were based. Second, the assessment report should indicate whether or not good arguments have been made to support any deviation from existing guidelines.

Experience within the PER Scheme

The PER Scheme is a voluntary scheme subscribed to by about 15 countries. The exchange of assessment reports within the PER Scheme is very important to member countries to facilitate their own assessment. It can give assurance that conclusions are based on the same notions, or provide a second opinion when faced with a difficult decision. In the Netherlands the exchange of assessment reports has also helped solve some outstanding problems by seeing how other countries have resolved the issues. However, it is the experience of the PER Scheme that the exchange of assessment reports does not necessarily expedite the review process. The challenge within the EU mutual recognition procedure is to use the assessment reports to enable authorities to complete their reviews within the prescribed 60 days.

Conclusion

The opportunity to exchange assessment reports can be beneficial, both in providing assurance and in bringing a new perspective to the review. The exchange and use of assessment reports, similar to that within the PER Scheme, is already operational within the European Union; it will evolve faster due to the binding legal situation. In the long run, the assessment report of the Reference Member State will be solely used for decision-making in other Member States.

In conclusion, there is no doubt that both the exchange of assessment reports and the training of assessors will improve the regulatory review process.

10 The regulatory assessment report in the new European system

KJELL STRANDBERG

Summary

1. The major challenge of the new system within the European Union (EU) for the licensing and follow-up of medicines rests with the regulators. Moving to central authorisations and mutual recognition of other agencies' assessments calls for a new mode of operation for the drug regulatory agencies.

2. The quality of the assessment report will be key to the success of the new EU system. Not only is there a need for a standardised format but also it is important that the assessment report reflects the full review process.

3. The audit trail within the assessment report should clearly explain how decisions have been reached; it will be essential to both applicants and other regulatory agencies and, ultimately, to the public.

4. Among the prerequisites for accomplishing a high quality assessment report, are up-to-date clinical guidelines and evaluation criteria in all therapeutic areas. In this regard, the current situation is far from optimal.

Introduction

With the introduction on 1st January 1995 of the new EU system for licensing and follow-up of new medicines the regulatory process is being revolutionised in Europe.

For most of its products the pharmaceutical industry can avail itself of the regulatory review process judged to be most efficient with respect to obtaining marketing authorisations, i.e. the central-ised procedure, the mutual recognition procedure or the national procedure. The choice of procedure will determine the number of possible simultaneous market introductions as well as failures. The choice of Reference Member State and proposal for rapporteur are highly likely to influence the course of the regulatory review process and its outcome.

Despite some of the uncertainties embodied in the system as viewed by industry, the major challenge rests with the regulators. Moving from a state where national marketing authorisations once were the results of sovereign decision-making, to Euro-authorisa-tions and mutual recognition of the assessments by other agencies calls for a completely new mode of operation for the drug regulatory agencies involved. The strict time limits imposed on the review processes add to this challenge.

Many of the potential obstacles to a smoothly operating system have been foreseen and steps have been taken in order to minimise them. Instrumental in this regard is the evolution of scientific consensus-making, a process that the Committee for Proprietary Medicinal Products (CPMP) has been engaged in over the years. As a result, the number of applications submitted either via the concer-tation procedure or the multistate procedure have increased steadily with time. The CPMP has produced technical guidelines on what documentation a company should submit in order to meet the formal criteria for a regulatory review in a number of product areas. Along with this work there has been an increasing understanding of the criteria for acceptable efficacy and safety adopted by the different Member States.

The assessment report

In order to maximise the possibilities for an efficient and accurate review process involving representatives from up to 15 EU regulatory agencies, a common standard for an assessment report was deemed an absolute prerequisite. Hence, prior to the introduction of the new system, a guideline for the format of an assessment report was elaborated, i.e. CPMP Guideline on the Assessment Report (AR), III 15447/94/EC. In part this built on the guideline produced earlier by the European Free Trade Association (EFTA) Pharmaceutical Evaluation Report (PER) Scheme.

Even if the requirements for the assessment report in the centralised procedure have not been finalised, in essence the guideline will also apply here. Apart from the need for a standard format accommodating the general characteristics as well as any particular features of a product, it is essential that the assessment report reflects the full review process, i.e. the fact that the completed assessment report has been preceded by a number of drafts, each in turn amended and/or updated in the light of new information from the applicant, regulatory authority, in-house discussions etc. This audit trail will explain how a proposal for marketing authorisation or rejection has been arrived at and as such is an indispensable element in the regulatory process, both to the applicant and to other regulatory agencies.

The assessment report is "the regulatory expert report" which shall comprise a critical, comprehensive but concise, analysis of the application. Not only shall the applicant's data be reviewed but also the applicant's expert reports and summaries as well as compliance with, or deviation from, CPMP guidelines, and the proposal for the Summary of Product Characteristics (SmPC) shall be taken fully into account.

The assessment report shall provide clear recommendations for approval or rejection of the application based on detailed benefit/risk considerations. If an authorisation is recommended to be subject to conditions, these should be set out.

If the assessment report serves the purposes outlined above it will make the important task of quality assurance (QA) review by

Table 10.1 Prerequisites for an efficient high quality European review process

- Adequate technical guidelines
- Well prepared submissions
- Common evaluation criteria
- Adherence to standard assessment report format
- Constructively critical reviewers
- In-house quality assurance programme
- Critical and concise quality assurance review by non-rapporteur CPMP members and concerned Member States
- Procedures for amending and updating of the assessment reports (audit trail)
- Commitment and "colleagueality"

the receiving CPMP members and Member States manageable. A common format for the assessment report is the only realistic way in the short time available to familiarise a non-rapporteur CPMP member or a concerned Member State with an application for a new product. In addition, if the assessment report has been subjected to a QA programme prior to release, this will further facilitate the recognition process.

Prerequisites for an efficient high quality European review process

Some of the prerequisites for accomplishing a high quality assessment report that will be acceptable to other CPMP members or Member States within the new system are listed in Table 10.1. Admittedly, the current situation is far from optimal in this regard. Many of the existing clinical guidelines are outdated and many therapeutic areas are not covered. Furthermore, common evaluation criteria for most therapeutic areas have not been established and it is questionable whether that issue will be remitted in the foreseeable future. The other factors mentioned are more immediately deliverable, provided

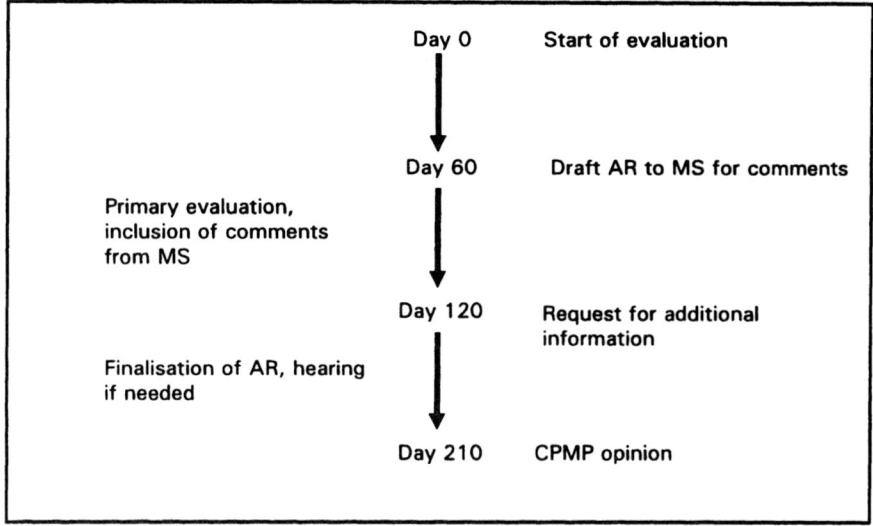

Day 0   Start of evaluation

Day 60   Draft AR to MS for comments

Primary evaluation,
inclusion of comments
from MS

Day 120   Request for additional
information

Finalisation of AR, hearing
if needed

Day 210   CPMP opinion

Figure 10.1 The review process for the centralised procedure in Europe.
AR = assessment report, MS = Member State

industry does its part and commitment to the cause prevails amongst
the regulators.

The making of an assessment report

During recent years most European regulatory authorities have
managed to cut their review times, thereby being prepared for
meeting the demands of the new system. Hence, the mutual recognition procedure is unlikely to cause a Reference Member State any
problems with regard to review deadlines. On the other hand, the
centralised procedure is more demanding in this respect as well, as
it calls for extensive consultations with the other CPMP members
and with the applicant.

Figure 10.1 gives the time frame for these consultations as well
as for the contributions by the CPMP itself. In this context it should
be emphasised that the draft assessment report offered for comments
at Day 60 is the result of a voluntary agreement between the CPMP
members and not a formal obligation. Moreover, the centralised

procedure rests on the premise that the non-rapporteur CPMP members shall not undertake an assessment of the dossier themselves, but only comment on the assessment report provided by the rapporteur and the co-rapporteur, respectively.

In Sweden, in order to cope with the new system should it be appointed rapporteur or co-rapporteur, the Medical Products Agency (MPA) has introduced a specific process to handle the centralised procedure and the mutual recognition procedure, respectively (Figures 10.2,3). Particular features are the appointment of project teams, early consultations with the applicant and early and continuous participation by the QA committees. Notably the external advisory expert body, the Board of Medicinal Products, will be consulted for mutual recognition applications but not for centralised procedure applications.

The audit trail

The draft assessment report shall list separately any major objections to issuing a marketing authorisation, as well as any points that need further clarification but which are not by themselves reasons for a rejection. This draft shall be scrutinised and constructively criticised by the receiving CPMP members and Member State drug regulatory agencies. In the new system only well-founded reasons for approval or rejection of an application are to be accepted. Any deficiencies in the documentation identified by the reviewing CPMP member or regulatory agency are to be "reviewed" for adequacy by the others. Similarly, this work should not be allowed to become an "add on" exercise, i.e. any new deficiencies proposed should be put to the same vigorous testing before being accepted. Apart from providing a full and concise assessment report, this process has the built-in function to serve as an educational tool and hence offer a mechanism for raising the overall standard of performance.

As for the centralised procedure, it is essential to ensure that the assessment report becomes properly updated when new data or explanations by the company arrive. Similarly, views put forward by CPMP members must be recorded and accommodated in the

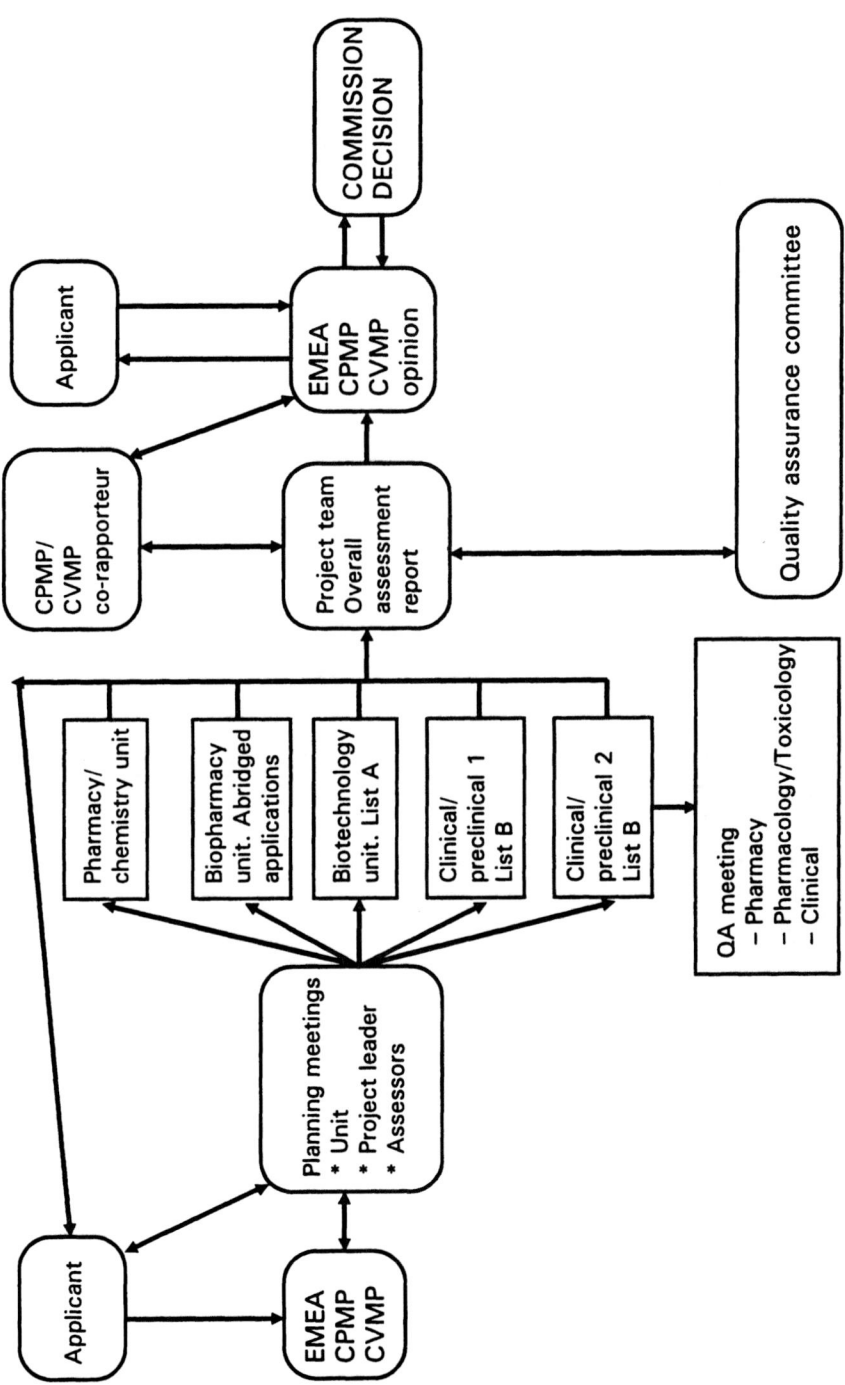

Figure 10.2 MPA assessment process for the centralised procedure

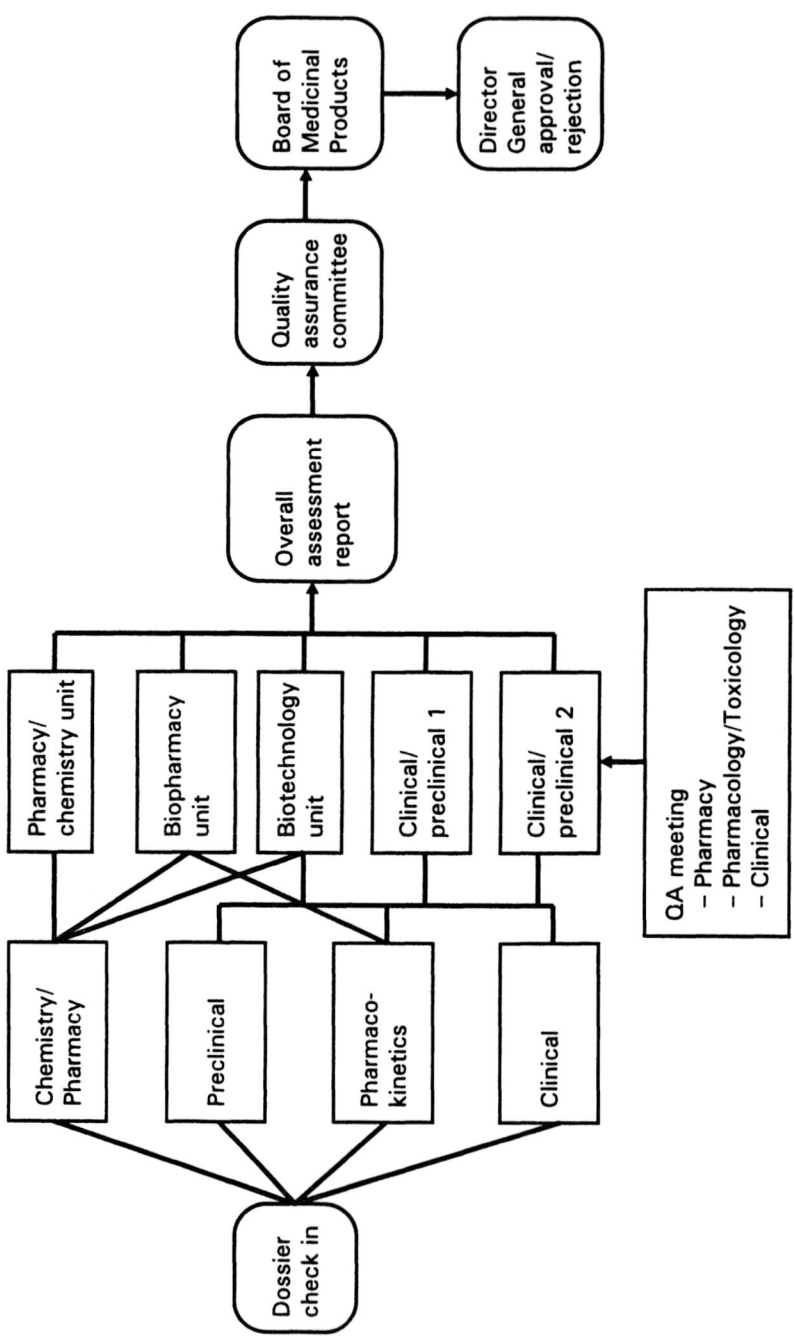

Figure 10.3 MPA national assessment process (for mutual recognition)

process. Unless this is done, there will be problems in tracking how decisions ultimately are shaped. This audit trail is of particular importance since the basis for each decision will eventually be publicly released. It must be recognised that the updated assessment report on which a CPMP opinion rests constitutes the core document for the European Public Assessment Report.

Conclusion

In summary, the quality of the assessment report, including adherence to the format agreed upon, is going to be one of the most important determining factors for the success of the new system.

11 Industry expert reports: An aid to the reviewer?

ROBERT TEMPLE

Summary

1. The value of summaries is not in doubt. Much of the guidance given by the European Community (EC) on how to prepare an expert report is similar to guidance the FDA gives to sponsors preparing submissions for review by the Food and Drug Administration.

2. What is unique, and hard for FDA staff to understand is the apparent deference given to the expert report when the expert is a sponsor, employee or paid consultant whose task is plainly to support approval. The FDA expects dossiers to be truthful but also expects that on matters of judgement, a sponsor-generated document will reflect the sponsor's interests. That interest will inevitably lie in supporting an application for marketing; the expert report cannot possibly reflect any other conclusion.

3. Although the expert report must be an advocacy document, it provides the sponsor with the opportunity to confront and explain any potential deficiencies in the application, a useful exercise and one that could well enhance the credibility of the application. Like every part of a dossier, however, the expert report must be considered in light of its content, not the "expertise" of its author.

Introduction

The Centre for Medicines Research showed considerable imagination in asking someone from the FDA who has actually seen only a few expert reports, to comment on their value. The opportunity, though, is welcome. The fact that the industry expert report has so much prestige and is treated with such deference and enthusiasm in Europe seems, on the face of it, rather strange on our side of the Atlantic. This is not to doubt the value of summaries, of which the expert is one kind. But anyone who prepares or reads summaries knows that they are highly selective documents, and can, by intent or inadvertently, be misleading or at least one-sided.

Although we, like the EC, would expect any summary from sponsors to be truthful, that is not the same as saying we would anticipate a neutral document. Any submission that is part of an application **must** be an advocacy document, useful to the extent that it summarises and explains complex data, but not an independent judgement. The identification of a report as an "expert" report seems to suggest willingness to rely on the judgement and expertise of the author. That, again, seems a puzzling deference to give to an agent of the commercial sponsor. Such an expert may have extraordinary credentials, but he is in no sense a neutral participant in the judgement about approval of the drug. On the other hand, properly interpreted, the expert report can undoubtedly make a contribution to the review. Before suggesting what that contribution is, I want to take note of the very substantial similarity between the guidance to sponsors preparing summaries (US) and the expert report (EC). The seeming distinction between the "factual" document sought in the USA and the "critical" document sought in the EC may be less than people imagine.

Much of the advice that the FDA and the EC give to sponsors preparing summaries, including expert reports, is very similar. The overviews, summaries and analyses required in regulations or requested in guidelines by the FDA are listed in Table 11.1. Although the new drug application summary (NDAS) is specifically expected to be a factual summary, there is unavoidably very substantial interpretation and emphasis. The integrated summaries of efficacy

Table 11.1 Overviews, summaries and analyses required or requested by the FDA

- Index (21 CFR 314.50 (b))

- Summary of the application (21 CFR 314.50(c))

- Integrated summary of data demonstrating substantial evidence of effectiveness and support for the recommended dose (21 CFR 314.50(d)(5)(v))

- Integrated summary of safety information updated 4 months after NDA submission and after receipt of approvable letter (21 CFR 314.50(d)(5)(vi))

- Integrated summary of the benefits and risks of the drug (21 CFR 314.50(d)(5)(viii))

- Background/overview of clinical investigations (guideline)

- Expert report on the clinical documentation

and safety are also highly interpretative. Also called for in FDA guidelines is a summary of benefits and risks, an important section when there are problems, such as a particularly serious adverse effect, an unusually small database, marginal or inconsistent evidence, use of an unusual surrogate endpoint, the very matters an expert report might take up.

The summary of the application is a document of 50–200 pages which should provide a good general understanding of the drug product and the application. It has its own guideline; this calls for an overview of the clinical studies that specifically addresses critical study design features. There is also a requirement to provide a table of controlled studies, short narratives on each study and an overall analysis of the studies; many of the same kinds of presentations and analyses, are requested in the expert report.

In the European system, the expert report on the clinical documentation is supposed to be short (25 pages) but it appears that appended tabular presentations make it a considerably larger document. In the clinical trials section a discussion of efficacy and safety is required with a focus on the most important studies, with particular attention to those trials which give unequivocal evidence of efficacy. The combination of narrative and tables is expected to give a very clear idea of the design of the critical trials, essentially the kind of description sought in the US application summary. The global analysis of efficacy and of safety called for in the expert report are largely descriptive, but there are requests for evaluation and explanation – why some trials failed, the pertinence of the studies (would the expert ever admit they were not pertinent?) and the therapeutic value (comparison with other therapies).

Comparison of the EC and the FDA

Table 11.2 provides a comparison of the main features of the summaries to be included in dossiers submitted to the FDA or the Committee for Proprietary Medicinal Products (CPMP). Summaries for the FDA are expected to be both factual and truthful, but they are not mere descriptions; there are many opportunities to make assess-

Table 11.2 Comparison of summary and analysis requirements. US and EC

	US	*EC*
Documents	NDAS, ISE ISS	Expert report
Author	Unspecified	Expert, qualified
Length	NDAS to 200 pages ISE, ISS, others not specified	25 pages and tables and individual summaries of important studies
Expectation	Factual, opinions identified; "bias" expected; truthfulness also expected	"Critical" review position taken; factual summary **not** sufficient, personal review of all data
Relation to detailed report	Cross-reference expected	Cross-reference expected
Presentation	Tables, figures	Tables, figures

NDAS – NDA summary
ISE – Integrated summary of effectiveness
ISS – Integrated summary of safety

ments. The agency presumes such assessments will have the bias of any interested party. By contrast, the expert report is supposed to be a critical review; the 1994 Draft Notice to Applicants states: "The expert is expected to take and defend a clear position on the product in the light of current scientific knowledge". But what does this really mean? It cannot mean the EC expects an unbiased assessment; it can only mean that the expert is expected to provide a sophisticated analysis of the data, including problems. It seems clear that the expert report is an advocacy document and I have no doubt that EC reviewers recognise this. It **must** favour approval and reflect the company view and it will not provide the reviewer with reasons for rejecting the application. Rather, it will explain why, **despite the flaws**, the data are acceptable.

Role of the expert report

The expert report appears to be the place where the sponsor can address those things about the application that are imperfect – serious adverse effects, other studies that could have been done but were not, uncertainties about doses, etc. – and explain why the drug merits approval anyway. For a number of reasons this has considerable practical value. First, it is bad policy to make the reviewer discover the flaws in the data; it makes the reviewer wonder even more than usual what else is lurking in the data. It is far better to reveal flaws and explain why they are unimportant. Second, the exercise of preparing a critical review probably has a salutary impact on the quality of the submission; looking for "holes" in the data will lead to a better dossier. Finally, the attempt to produce a critical report, to anticipate a reviewer's concerns, should decrease the "attitudinal gap" between the submitter and the regulatory reviewer. Acknowledgement that the data are not perfect is a useful attitude that will lead to better communication with the reviewer.

Deciding who should be the expert is an interesting question. The entire development of a drug is carried out by in-house and external experts. They are more familiar with the details of study design, the choices made among alternatives, what other drug companies have done, and most other aspects of the dossier than any external newly-arrived expert could be. On the other hand, a fresh look, with fresh insight and no investment in the programme may give a better chance of anticipating the questions a regulator might have.

Conclusions

Any excellent summary can help the reviewer and the value of the expert report as a type of summary is clear. It may be particularly helpful in providing an opportunity for the company to explain the potential deficiencies of the application. The expert review, however, no matter how distinguished the expert, is an advocacy document. If the expert, whether sponsor –employed or external, had not found the dossier adequate, the expert report would not have been submitted . . . another would be found. The expert report must therefore be evaluated on the basis of its content, not the level of distinction of the expert.

12 The use of internal and external experts and advisory boards: The European experience

GORM JENSEN

Summary

1. The Danish Medical Agency relies on external experts, employing just one full-time, in-house medical expert. Medical assessors are also part-time clinicians, whereas expert members of advisory boards have full-time clinical/scientific duties. *Ad hoc* experts are recruited for working parties etc.

2. The advantage of external, as compared to internal, experts is the maintenance of expertise. The disadvantages include the unpredictability of the quality of review, competing demands on their time, expense, and a tendency to develop interests which jeopardise their expert status.

3. Within the European Community there are major outstanding issues concerning experts. Their qualifications should be documented and universally recognised. Standardised recruitment procedures, open to scrutiny, are needed and the training and maintenance of experts should become a priority matter in the European Community.

Introduction

The use of external experts and advisory boards has been proposed as a way of assisting regulatory authorities in dealing with a large volume of work in a shorter space of time, and of ensuring appropriate expert opinion on a wide range of issues. In this paper, the definition of an expert within the regulatory process is discussed, together with their role, tasks, recruitment and training, with particular reference to the experience of Denmark.

The role of experts

Although widely recognised as a person having special skill and knowledge, an expert within the context of the regulatory process is not clearly defined. There are no specific requirements for education, qualifications or experience. Within Europe it would appear that an expert is anyone who is considered to be an expert by their national authority; the only formal requirement is a declaration of interest.

There is a demand for experts at all stages of the regulatory process from pre-registration, where background requirements for applicants are needed, through licensing, to the post-marketing maintenance of licensing requirements and pharmacovigilance. In practical terms experts can contribute to the preparation of guidelines for industry and regulatory authorities, prepare assessment reports, and interpret scientific or clinical knowledge and data from a regulatory perspective (e.g. pharmacovigilance data).

The role of the expert, however, is solely to give expert advice; there should be no opportunity for exercising a hidden agenda (career, financial or more subtle interests). This is important at the national level and even more so in an international context such as, for instance, the European Community (EC) assessment.

The Danish model

The Danish Medical Agency is comparatively small, employing about 140 people of whom only 10 or 12 are involved in the registration process as part-time medical assessors. The Danish system is

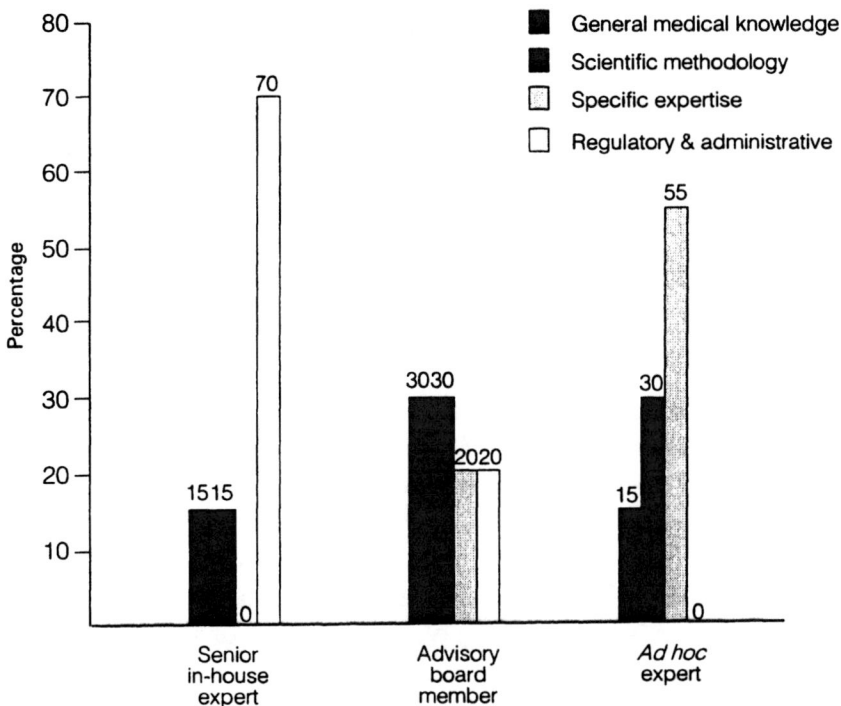

Figure 12.1 Professional profiles of experts

very different from others in that no one in the Agency is able to make scientifically-based decisions on their own; all the scientists are either part-time medical assessors or members of a regulatory advisory board with professional commitments elsewhere. Regulatory decisions are therefore taken by outside experts!

There is undoubtedly a requirement for different types of external expert with differing professional profiles (Figure 12.1). In Denmark, part-time medical assessors are recruited, through advertising, from doctors at the senior registrar level. Advisory board members are hand-picked from medical assessors who have reached a senior level or from *ad hoc* experts who have gained some regulatory experience. *Ad hoc* experts themselves are usually prominent figures within their field, recruited for participation in working groups and certain specific tasks. In addition there is a role for in-house experts at a senior level who have acquired specific regulatory and administrative expertise.

As time goes on, however, all experts lose their expertise; the period of usefulness as an expert is limited. The professional profile of the in-house medical assessor will change as specific knowledge is lost; their useful period might be 4–6 years. Even the expert member of an advisory board has a finite period of usefulness, perhaps around 10 years.

Maintaining experts

Full-time internal experts cannot be maintained as experts. However, the period of transition from expert to regulator may perhaps be prolonged through participation in clinical and scientific courses and other initiatives.

Medical assessors should continue as part-time clinicians; their participation in scientific studies is to be encouraged since "hands-on" experience is the best way of keeping up to date with scientific knowledge. It is inevitable, and desirable, that they should work in clinical trials sponsored by pharmaceutical companies; however, they should not be employed by industry. Continued education for medical assessors is necessary in topics such as assessment methodology and regulatory requirements. A process for training as well as continued education is needed within the EC.

By contrast, members of advisory boards can continue with their full-time clinical or scientific duties and thus maintain their expert status.

Experts: advantages and disadvantages

The undoubted advantage of using experts is the provision of expert knowledge, much needed in the regulatory process. In this context part-time external experts are preferred in Denmark since they do not lose their expertise, and maintain themselves better than in-house experts. External experts often work faster but their time is in much demand.

Experts are only human; they have their limitations, too. Many lack administrative discipline and therefore work too slowly, often with total disregard for the (bureaucratic) regulatory process. In some countries they are expensive. Most assessors burn out after a few years, and many develop interests in moral, ethical or political issues relating to regulatory medicine which is a sign of impending burn-out, and this renders them of little value as experts.

Regarding the quality of a review, this is always predictable from the in-house expert, who is conveniently located at the regulatory agency. By contrast, external experts may either produce brilliant reviews or useless pontifications. Frequently their work needs editing by the in-house expert.

Experts in the EC

Up to now, experts have been put at the disposal of the EC by individual national authorities. Inevitably this results in lack of standardisation. There are a number of major outstanding issues concerning experts in the Community regulatory process which need to be addressed and these include the following: the criteria for expertise are lacking; no established channels for recruitment; no clear definition of role; and no responsibility for training and maintaining experts.

The qualifications of experts should be objective, documented, verifiable and universally recognised. Standardised recruitment procedures for experts are needed which are open and amenable to critical review, and which allow for an element of competition so that the best experts are chosen.

Regulatory experts are a resource, which should be carefully guarded; their training and maintenance must become a priority matter within the EC. Development of a *modus operandi* for experts, together with a consideration of inducement and discipline, could also aid their function within the regulatory process.

13 Highlights of the Pharmaceutical Research and Manufacturers Association proposal for FDA reform

DAVID R SAVELLO

Summary

1.   The Pharmaceutical Research and Manufacturers Association (PhRMA) undertook a programme to develop concepts and designs for the purpose of advising the US Congress on reforming the regulatory processes involved in drug development and approval in the USA.

2.   Proposed reforms focus primarily on clinical research and the drug approval process and seek to eliminate unnecessary and outdated laws and regulations that are delaying drug development and approvals while not providing any greater assurance of safety.

3.   The reforms, if enacted, will create a scientific and management oversight of the Food and Drug Administration (FDA), allow for external organisations to participate in the drug review process, strengthen the advisory committee process, and bring the regulatory requirements in line with state of the art scientific and statistical standards.

Introduction

In early 1995, the Pharmaceutical Research and Manufacturers Association began work on a proposal to make recommendations to the US Congress for legislative changes to reform the drug review and approval process in the United States. The goal was to improve the drug development approval system in order to get innovative new medicines to patients faster and more efficiently while assuring their safety. The regulatory problems surrounding new drug review and approval appear to be unique to the US system. Data support the observation that there is no measurable benefit of safety to the United States population as a result of the continuing lag of innovative drug introduction to the US marketplace compared to the other major markets. Also Kaitin *et al.* (1995) identified additional problems with the drug development and approval process.

In developing a set of recommendations for legislative changes, PhRMA formed a panel of experts made up of former FDA commissioners and a deputy commissioner and headed by the former Chairman of the House Subcommittee on Health and the Environment, The Honorable Paul G Rogers. The panel assisted in developing the concepts for reform. The "Rogers Group" report of recommendations was then incorporated into the proposal along with input from PhRMA's Science and Regulatory Section, Regulatory Affairs Co-ordinating Committee, FDA Reform Key Issues Team, and the PhRMA Board.

A team of member companies' regulatory affairs executives, lawyers, chief executive officers and consultants were assigned to provide design of the concepts of FDA reform. The design reflected the concepts and incorporated key elements of the Rogers Group recommendations. Legislative language was drafted to reflect concept designs. This paper summarises some of the highlights of the output from these committees. The PhRMA believes that legislatively implementing these changes will result in a more rapid and more cost-effective drug development and approval process without any compromise in safety.

Mission

Although the FDA was established by legislation in 1938, that legislation failed to contain a mission statement. The proposal adds a mission statement relating to drugs, devices and biological products which reflects a balance between promoting and protecting the health of the American people. The FDA should promote health by facilitating the timely availability of safe and effective products, and the FDA should protect health by taking prompt and appropriate action to prevent public health risk.

Policy and performance panel

Although there have been independent and government commissions to review the policy and performance of the FDA, there is no permanent organisation that performs this function. As a result, FDA performance is subject to only periodic *ad hoc* review and there is neither a consistent policy oversight nor any follow-up to assure that needed changes are in fact undertaken by the agency. This section establishes a permanent policy and performance review panel to provide a consistent and detailed oversight of all aspects of FDA activities.

Good manufacturing practice

Presently, FDA field personnel through the pre-approval inspection can withhold approval of a new drug for technical reasons and minor good manufacturing practice (GMP) violations. This section prevents field personnel from reversing the opinions of and decisions of the new drug application (NDA) reviewers and that before the FDA can take action to delay or prevent the marketing of a drug because of GMP issues, the agency must find that the violation has caused the drug to have a serious safety, sterility, bioequivalence, etc. problem.

The content and review of an NDA

Presently, NDAs constitute hundreds of volumes of documents, most of these being raw data listings and case report forms. This section allows submission of certified reports of studies on safety and effectiveness supported by tables of the relevant data and would not be required to include tabulations of all of the raw data or case report forms except for deaths and dropouts due to adverse reactions. Only the Office Director would have the authority to request the submission of data line listings and case report forms in a particular instance.

The proposal also directs the FDA to utilise outside organisations or individuals with the appropriate expertise to review NDAs whenever that is effective and efficient to do so and the applicant has agreed. Further, standards will be established relating to promptness, technical excellence, lack of bias, and a knowledge of regulatory and scientific standards for the review of all NDAs.

Manufacturing changes

Most manufacturing changes require prior approval by the FDA before the changes can be implemented. This can often take years to achieve, is costly and is an unnecessary burden on the manufacturer. This section allows for changes that do not change the formulation or release specifications, to be made at any time and reported on an annual basis. Other changes can also be made at any time, but also require a study demonstrating equivalence and must be reported through a supplement or amendment submitted at the time the change is made.

Clinical research

The FDA currently requires that all clinical investigations be conducted only after submission of an investigational new drug (IND) plan to the agency containing detailed and exhaustive information about the drug and prior animal and human studies on it. This section allows clinical research to proceed on the basis of summary reports of basic information 5 days after this information is received by the FDA. In addition, to minimise the number and length of "clinical holds", the agency would only be allowed to administer clinical holds if the FDA determined that the drug represents an unreasonable risk to the safety of the patients.

New drug approval standard

Under current law, there must be substantial evidence of effectiveness defined as evidence consisting of adequate and well-controlled clinical investigations conducted by qualified experts. Because of the lack of precision in this definition, the FDA has generally required at least two adequate and well-controlled clinical trials and on occasion has said that one such trial will suffice. This section proposes that substantial evidence of effectiveness requires data from one well-controlled clinical investigation as long as there is confirmatory evidence in the form of scientifically sound data obtained before or after the well-controlled investigation. It also relies heavily on the judgement of qualified experts to evaluate the effectiveness of the drug.

Expedited review of new drugs

This section establishes a procedure under which new drugs that are first reviewed and approved by these organisations will receive an expedited review within the FDA provided the applicant has already submitted a full NDA for that drug. Once the drug has been reviewed and approved by the European Medicines Evaluation Agency (EMEA), the United Kingdom Medicines Control Agency (MCA), or any other competent non-governmental organisation approved by the FDA and meets the same type of standards for reviewing and approving new drugs, the complete dossier or other submission made to that organisation may be submitted to the FDA. Within 180 days of receipt of the NDA, or 90 days of receipt of the submission mentioned above, whichever is later, the FDA must either approve the drug or disapprove it. The sole basis for disapproval is that the drug has been demonstrated to be unsafe or ineffective.

Advisory committee review

To remedy some of the existing problems with the advisory committee process, this section mandates that the advisory committee process be administered by the Office of the Commissioner independent of the centres that regulate drugs and biologics. A sponsor shall have the right to advisory committee review of scientific decisions by FDA and scientific issues pending before the FDA, including issues of science policy. The FDA would be required to make a final decision on matters relating to prescription drugs within 30 days after the committee has rendered its advice. The make-up of the committees would also be designed in order to assure that sufficient expertise is available to the committee on the particular matter that is scheduled to come before the advisory committee at any given meeting.

Dissemination of scientific information

Under this section manufacturers would be allowed to distribute articles that contain information not in the approved package insert if they appear in independent peer-reviewed medical textbooks, certain journals, and compendia. The journals are those of the medical societies associated with medical specialty certifying boards or equivalent organisations in health economics and other journals designated by the Commissioner. Such reprints could only be distributed accompanied by a copy of the package insert and a statement that the article includes information not approved by the FDA. This section also prevents the FDA from halting the use of information about approved uses, or any pharmacoeconomic information unless the agency found the misuse of such information would likely cause the drug to be used in a way that is unsafe or ineffective.

Right to review by expert advisory panel

This allows a sponsor to obtain a review of a drug for serious or life-threatening conditions by a scientific review group and that this review be completed with a recommendation within 120 days. If the scientific review group recommends approval, the application is automatically deemed approved in 60 days unless the FDA finds that approval would create an unreasonable risk to public health or safety or the product will not be manufactured in accordance with good manufacturing practices.

Reference

Kaitin KI *et al.* (1995). *Drug Information Journal,* **29**: 361–373.

14 Suggestions that might be considered for improving the review process

Cyndy Lumley

Summary

1. Several suggestions for overcoming the problems experienced by industry or regulators in achieving an efficient regulatory review were made by the workshop participants. The overriding theme was increased partnership between the regulators and the pharmaceutical industry, and there was agreement that five general areas require further discussion: the size of the dossier, dialogue, the review process itself, company strategies and specialised procedures such as mutual recognition or interactive submissions.

2. The participants agreed that one aim should be to reduce substantially the size of the dossier, particularly the clinical section. This will require collaboration between industry and regulators, and will be assisted by the ongoing ICH discussions.

3. Authorities can learn from each other and industry in order to re-engineer the review process, and there is an onus on industry to improve the quality of their submissions and respond to questions in an efficient and timely manner. The participants agreed that a long-term goal should be to move to a transnational system that consists of a single submission and a prompt, uniform decision.

Throughout the workshop, the presentations and discussion focused on problems experienced by industry or regulators in achieving an efficient regulatory review. Many suggestions for overcoming these problems were made by the participants, which were discussed in some detail in syndicate groups. The overriding theme was increased partnership between the regulators and the pharmaceutical industry, who should be working closely together while recognising that each has different roles and responsibilities.

In the time available it was not possible to produce a mutually agreed list of specific actions which could be taken by either industry or regulators to improve the review process. However, there was agreement that five general areas require further discussion: the size of the dossier, dialogue, the review process itself, company strategies and specialised procedures such as mutual recognition or interactive submissions (Tables 14.1–3).

Size of the dossier

The size of the dossier submitted in support of a marketing authorisation has increased such that many now constitute hundreds of volumes of documents, a large proportion of these being raw data listings and case report forms. There was considerable discussion on the possible reasons for the increase in size, with a general consensus that sponsors and regulators had both contributed to the problem. As more data are offered by industry, so more is requested by the regulatory authorities, a process referred to as "regulatory creep". According to some industry representatives, much of the so-called regulatory creep is sponsor-generated, perhaps to atone for imperfect experimental designs at the outset. Furthermore, global development means that studies are done in Europe, the USA and Japan, resulting in a large database, and the way in which this information is put into the dossier requires examination. As one regulator pointed out, although more data are being provided, the information on which the authorities make their decisions is not changing.

The participants agreed that one aim should be to reduce substantially the size of the dossier, and that the clinical part is the major

Table 14.1 Suggestions to improve the review process, for consideration by industry

Examine ways to reduce the size of the dossier by:

- Focusing on relevant data;

- Assessing whether all studies need to be conducted or included in full;

- Making the dossier more user-friendly by integrating information.

Improve dialogue and feedback by:

- Identifying, pursuing and utilising all possible avenues of communication with authorities;

- Providing feedback to reviewers on the questions raised;

- Seeking ways to share general regulatory feedback with other companies.

Help to re-engineer the review process by:

- Sharing re-engineering methodology and experiences in drug development, with regulatory authorities;

- Assisting work-load planning by indicating in advance the number of future applications.

Address internal inefficiency by:

- Developing regulatory intelligence and know-how;

- Anticipating questions at an early stage and providing answers within the dossier;

- Reducing company response times.

issue. Several suggestions as to how this might be addressed were raised for further discussion.

Focus on relevant data

The dossier should include only "critical" data – that which is essential to demonstrate the quality, safety and efficacy of a new medicine. Several regulators expressed the view that industry

Table 14.2 Suggestions to improve the review process, for consideration by authorities

Improve dialogue and feedback by:

- Establishing and publishing formal mechanisms for dialogue and feedback;

- Organising workshops to discuss examples of best/worst practice by companies and by reviewers;

- Seeking ways to increase dialogue between agencies.

Re-engineer the review process by:

- Identifying transparent defined stages and benchmarking across authorities;

- Publishing clear performance targets;

- Establishing a quality assurance process.

Help to improve response to questions by:

- Developing better methods for training of reviewers to ensure questions are appropriate;

- Benchmarking questions across authorities;

- Defining a maximum time limit for industry response.

regard many more data as 'essential' than do the authorities; the dossier therefore includes an excess of information added because sponsors are exploring issues other than supporting the case for marketing authorisation, for example, marketing, pricing, health economics, or entrance to formularies. It is necessary to assess whether such information needs to be generated at the pace at which it is today, or if it is available at the time of a marketing submission, whether it could be presented in a different way, for example, as a summary. Furthermore, there can be a considerable amount of unnecessary repetition in reports from one study to another, and there is a need for industry to address this and to focus on the important results.

Table 14.3 Suggestions to improve the review process, which require further discussion between authorities and industry

Examine ways to reduce the size of the dossier by:

- Discussing the possibility of excluding individual patient case report forms from the dossier;

- Including only completed study reports with group means and out-liers, rather than all the raw data;

- Agreeing a strategy for clinical design using scientific principles, so that only the key variables relevant to safety, quality and efficacy are examined.

Consider specialised review procedures such as:

- Conditional approvals;

- Interactive submissions.

Move towards a transnational system by:

- Considering mutual recognition of part of the dossier;

- Taking into account prior approvals in other countries.

It is essential to assess the regulatory requirements and ascertain the real needs of agencies and reviewers, as all information received by an agency must be examined. One suggestion was that the dossier should include only the completed study reports with group means and outliers, and not necessarily all of the raw data. Consideration should also be given to excluding individual case report forms from the dossier.

Agree a strategy for clinical design

It was suggested that there is a need to be more creative regarding clinical research methodology, and that this requires further discussion between industry and regulators. It is important to use scientific principles to define the key variables, to reduce the numbers of patients and studies, and to avoid generating information that is not relevant to the purpose of the studies. For example, according to one regulator, small open label Phase IIIB studies have little value, unless they can be brought together in further analyses. However, they constitute quite a large proportion of the dossier.

Make the dossier user-friendly

Several regulators emphasised the need to integrate the information in the dossier, rather than presenting separate reports. It was suggested that the dossier should have a hierarchical structure, with prioritisation of the information, and one way to achieve this might be to define a "model" report. The move towards electronic dossiers might also help, as they have real advantages for the regulators in that it is easier to extract information.

Improve dialogue and feedback

There are many opportunities for agency/industry communication during the development process, during review and in the post-approval phase. Dialogue requires careful planning and effective management, and many suggestions were raised as to how industry and authorities might improve and increase dialogue, both prior to and during the review process.

Dialogue between company and authority

Several industry representatives suggested that proactive networking with regulatory authorities will allow a faster review, whilst the regulators encouraged companies to identify, pursue and utilise all possible avenues of communication. Companies should establish contact with authorities early in the development process, particularly with the primary reviewer, but should hold back from asking for too much. There was a suggestion that formal mechanisms of dialogue and interaction between authority and company are desirable to ensure consistency. To achieve this, it would be helpful if authorities would publish the ground rules and empower individuals to talk to companies.

Open meetings on issues of difficulty for both parties ('hot' topics) would be useful, and a joint approach to the training of employees would be beneficial to both the agencies and industry by raising overall standards and so developing a pool of more informed and capable regulatory professionals. Many participants advocated regular workshops or reviewer feedback sessions to discuss examples of best/worst practice. This is already happening in Japan, where the Ministry of Health and Welfare holds sessions with companies twice a year, based on a list of generic questions and answers compiled by the reviewers. It was also suggested that feedback from companies to regulators on the questions raised, i.e. were they reasonable or unreasonable, might be helpful.

A common procedure between authorities for feedback would be beneficial, such as agreeing to send assessment reports to companies (with the recommendations on approval deleted). This would allow companies to begin to work on the obvious questions and there may be an opportunity to interact with an expert committee at an early stage.

Dialogue between competent authorities

According to one regulator, dialogue and interaction amongst the regulatory agencies may be of more advantage to industry over the next few years than dialogue between the agency and industry within a particular regime. Agencies should be seeking ways of sharing the results, data, analyses and ultimately the decisions – as industry globalises, agencies have to globalise as well.

Suggestions for more immediate opportunities for dialogue between competent authorities included holding workshops on best practice approaches to the review, agreeing the structure and content of the assessment report, exchanging information on the knowledge, skills and attitude required to be a competent assessor, and giving consideration to the possibility of joint training of assessors to ensure standard evaluation criteria for dossiers.

Dialogue between companies

There was considerable discussion on how information provided by regulators to specific companies might be made more generic. Many authorities spend considerable time giving advice to individual companies, but others who also need to know that information have great difficulty in obtaining it unless a guidance document is written. The sharing of this information would require a change in attitude on the part of the companies to allow, for example, minutes to be more widely available, open meetings on general subjects or specific sharing of experiences, or consensus meetings.

Re-engineer the review process

Re-engineering is not simply adding more resources, it is the idea of doing the right things rather than doing things right. Industry experience demonstrates that process improvement can pay large dividends, and the concepts could be applied to the review process and across the industry/agency interface.

Benchmark across authorities

It was suggested that authorities should carry out a 'work-flow' analysis to see where time is being wasted in the process. Several participants advocated the identification of transparent, defined stages which could be benchmarked across authorities. This might allow clear performance targets for each part of the review to be published by individual authorities, as industry experience has shown that the setting and review of joint targets will drive towards quicker reviews.

Establish quality assurance for the review process

Several regulators stressed the need for an effective quality assurance process within each agency, to ensure consistency of review within and across authorities. This is becoming more important, as in the future fewer authorities will be assessing the dossiers. Part of this might involve setting up a 'peer review' system or a performance review panel to provide a consistent and detailed oversight of each authority.

Establish electronic tracking systems

The Canadian authority is working towards a tracking system that can be accessed directly by the sponsor so that they can easily identify the stage in the review process their compound has reached. This will assist the sponsor and avoid the reviewer spending time tracking compounds, and it was suggested that other authorities should give consideration to this type of system.

Improve workload planning

It was suggested that industry could assist agencies in their workload planning by indicating in advance the number of future applications, or through the sharing of resource analysis and planning techniques.

Improve company strategy

It is clear that there are significant differences in the time to market depending on how companies plan their regulatory strategy for individual products. The industry participants were encouraged to set consistent and challenging targets, supported by a development plan in line with all available regulatory intelligence. The importance of developing regulatory intelligence and know-how was stressed, as thorough knowledge of regulatory systems and procedures will improve the quality of a dossier and the efficiency of a review. It was suggested that much of the onus for change rests with the industry, and Professor Lou Lasagna was quoted – "the ultimate NDAs are essentially self-reviewing, because all the important questions have been addressed".

Two aspects regarding questions were discussed: how to ensure that questions raised by reviewers are appropriate, and the need to reduce company response time.

Ensure questions are appropriate

Several participants emphasised the need to ensure that inappropriate questions are not sent to companies by inexperienced regulators. This can contribute to regulatory creep, or increase the total review time if the company has to argue its case as to why the question is not relevant. It was suggested that benchmarking the questions across authorities, appropriate training of reviewers and the implementation of a quality assurance process within authorities might begin to address this problem. Companies can also help by anticipating questions at an early stage and providing answers within the dossier.

Reduce company response time

Several regulators pointed out that they are working at reducing primary response and review times, and it is demoralising for them if companies do not respond quickly to questions. There is a clear need for companies to identify the reasons for internal delays, and two participants described their experience in setting up a 'query response system', whereby questions and answers are logged and made available to all subsidiaries. This avoids any duplication of effort when the same questions are raised in different countries. It was also suggested that regulators could help companies by setting clear time limits for company response.

Consider specialised review procedures

There was considerable discussion concerning the pros and cons of conditional approvals and interactive submissions. The general consensus was that they should be considered in special circumstances, or if they would clearly speed up the review process.

Conditional approvals

The view was expressed that conditional approvals should be used more widely where minor issues can be resolved readily, and that they are important if the demonstration of efficacy is based on surrogate markers. However, several questions need to be addressed – is it correct to authorise a medicine when there are still significant questions unanswered, how does one enforce the conditions, what should be done if the conditions cannot be met? Some regulators suggested that it is incumbent upon the industry to show that the real endpoint that is looked for is satisfied by proper post-marketing surveillance, but it must be possible for clinical studies to deliver the conditions set.

Interactive submissions

Certain parts of the dossier are complete entities at an earlier stage than the clinical section, and the participants discussed whether or not it would be helpful to review these when they are available, prior to the final submission. It was agreed that this should only be considered if it speeds up the final review. There are some possible negative aspects to this, as therapeutic candidates may still be terminated and review at an early stage would be a waste of resources. Furthermore, this would put a large burden on industry as questions would be raised that might well be answered later in the development of the drug and it could result in an over-emphasis on negative preclinical findings if the clinical data are not available.

Future goals

The participants agreed that a long-term goal should be to move to a transnational system that consists of one submission with a prompt, unified decision. Considerable progress has already been made through mutual recognition (Europe) and shared reviews (PER Scheme). These have demonstrated the willingness for regulators to accept summaries produced by colleagues rather than reading every word in a submission. Many participants were of the opinion that prior approval in other countries should be taken into account more in the review. For example, if a new medicine was approved in Europe, it may not require such a rigorous review in the USA. However, it was suggested that it is not appropriate for sponsors to pose the day to day solutions, but it is up to the regulators to determine what works, what is acceptable, and what is not.

To simply mandate that the entire dossier should be mutually recognised is not feasible in the near future, but there are sections that might be considered for certain degrees of mutual recognition. A stepwise approach was suggested, perhaps starting with the preclinical or chemistry sections. The preclinical sections are the least controversial in terms of geographic interpretation and therefore might be the ideal element to propose for a pilot mutual recognition or joint review scheme.

Conclusions

Both regulatory and industry participants recognised that they should not lose sight of their collective mission: the improvement of the public health by the rapid introduction and application of safe and effective medicines. By focusing on those factors which contribute to the time spent on regulatory review, an important component of drug development time, it was possible to identify problem areas and suggest ways for improvement. As industry and regulatory representatives alike considered their future strategies, emphasis was placed on the need for partnership to encourage quick, efficient and credible reviews. The value of increased use of information technology, improved training of assessors, meetings and workshops, and standard evaluation criteria was recognised.

There is much that the authorities can learn from each other and from industry in order to re-engineer the review process. Equally, there is an onus on industry to improve the quality of their submissions and to respond to questions in an efficient and timely manner. However, one of the main points to arise from these discussions is the need to reduce the size of the clinical dossier. This will require collaboration between industry and regulators, and will be assisted by the ongoing ICH discussions, to which there should be continued commitment by both parties.

15 The ideal future regulatory system: An industry perspective

EVE E SLATER

Summary

1. In an ideal regulatory system there would be one submission, with a prompt, unified decision; and the system itself would be responsive, economical and complete. Inherent in such a system would be a single worldwide development programme predicated upon thoroughly articulated guidelines.

2. Much has been accomplished by industry in concert with the authorities in recent years towards such a Utopia, but problems remain. There is a need for a more rapid integration of scientific technology into drug development by both sponsors and assessors. The issue of harmonised dossier requirements has yet to be achieved and more emphasis must be placed on paperless submissions.

3. Future challenges may be even more daunting. Demands for prompt access to safe therapies are ever increasing, as will be pressure to develop, review and approve agents from novel therapeutic classes. With research and development costs spiralling, healthcare resource limitations will necessitate data on health economic outcomes. The way in which pharmacological agents are developed and regulated will be increasingly questioned by patient and taxpayer.

4. There is a need for all involved to meet and compromise, and not to lose sight of the collective mission: improvement of the public health by rapid introduction and application of medical advances.

"Dream unfettered by the dawn." (Stephen Foster, 1858)

Dream or possibility?

An ideal regulatory system from the point of view of both sponsor and regulator would be prompt and responsive. It would be both succinct and complete. It would, in my opinion, be paperless and it would be economical – or at least not more resource intensive than the system of today. Inherent in such a system would be a single worldwide development programme with common protocols being executed simultaneously across the three geographic areas. There would be one submission, a mutually recognised certification of compliance, a unified prompt decision based solely upon sound scientific principles and a single worldwide SmPC (Summary of Product Characteristics). All questions to the sponsor would be good questions; that is, predicated upon a clear understanding of the dossier and the data. All answers would be forthright, direct and prompt.

All development programmes would be formulated on established, proactively defined and thoroughly articulated guidelines, including ones for breakthrough therapeutic classes. Dialogue would be easily accessed, both formal and informal, beginning early in the process and with consistency as the rule. The reviewers would receive credit for their reviews, each of which requires definitive understanding of a therapeutic class. Lastly, the public, whom we all serve, would be most appreciative of these efforts.

Achievements

What problems toward achieving this ideal remain and how can they be solved? What future problems lie in wait? Despite the daunting nature of the task, substantial progress has been accomplished towards attainment of these collective goals within recent years. The very existence of this meeting with its respected participants bodes well for future progress.

While appreciable differences still exist between Western authorities and Japan, these differences have, for the most part, been recognised and discussed. Furthermore, the Ministry of Health and Welfare (MHW) has made substantial efforts to harmonise in areas of quality and safety. The European authorities have set a standard for benchmarking, have provided much encouragement to improve the efficiency of the review process and, in my judgement, have energised the International Conference on Harmonisation (ICH) process. The Food and Drug Administration (FDA) has clearly created a precedent for dialogue which is now being adopted throughout the world and by their utilisation, accelerated review processes have elevated the concept of prioritisation to beneficial heights.

Clearly, industry, for its part, has also accomplished much in concert with the authorities. Within the last decade, it has shown how to save lives of patients with heart failure, hypercholesterolaemia and ischaemic heart disease. Breakthrough therapies for depression, organ transplantation, haematological diseases, and certain forms of cancer have been contributed. Moreover, the concept of self-diagnosis and self-cure has progressed to empower patients in certain areas to treat self-limiting gastric hypersecretory conditions through the use of over-the-counter drugs of the H_2-receptor antagonist class. Now, work goes on as researchers continue to struggle with those major impediments to disease-free life: immunodeficiency syndrome, malignancy, and senescence.

Current problems and potential solutions

What can we do to facilitate the development and review process? Current problems have been summarised (Table 15.1) for which there are potential solutions (Table 15.2). More rapid integration of scientific technology into drug development by both developers and assessors is critical. The assessment of drug metabolism is ripe for change. Metabolic pathways can be predicted by the use of *in vitro* human microsomes. Similarly, potential drug:drug and drug:environment interactions could be defined *in vitro*. Science has advanced

Table 15.1 Current problems

1.	Less than optimal integration of scientific advances into review of dossiers.
2.	Incomplete harmonisation of submission requirements, compliance qualifications, review processes and labelling.
3.	Escalating research and development requirements and costs.
4.	Information explosion/excessive duplication.

to allow the use of *in vitro* expression systems for the human P450 drug metabolising enzymes. Emphasis should be placed on *in vivo* pharmacokinetic and pharmacodynamic studies to establish minimal effective dose and to better define gender, age, ethnic, and environmental effects (Harris, Benet and Schwartz, 1995; Spielberg, 1995).

In the area of toxicology, according to newly established scientific principles, improvement of the carcinogenicity bioassay is long overdue and such change has been championed repeatedly by the Centre for Medicines Research (CMR) (McAuslane, Lumley and Walker, 1992).

The field of biostatistics has matured, providing phenomenal clarity to data analysis. Reviewing bodies worldwide must be conscientious in both adopting and accepting these techniques (Zeger and Liang, 1986). Further, the growing body of pharmaco-epidemiological data contained in databases now available on line, should be applied to facilitate the attribution of adverse experiences (Strom and Carson, 1990). This would enable more meaningful labelling advice. Historic databases from well-powered, adequately sized epidemiological studies and/or meta-analyses, could conceivably be used to provide historical controls or to replace the need for some less valuable drug comparison studies (Gould *et al.*, 1995; Peto, 1990). In some cases, observational data can be used to resolve heretofore difficult-to-answer questions (Simon, Wagner and Vonkorff, 1995).

The concept of combining a Phase IIb with a Phase III study for pivotal registration has been raised. The distinction between Phases

Table 15.2 Potential solutions

1. More rapid integration of scientific advances into regulatory process, e.g.:
    –   Use *in vitro* studies to better define metabolic pathways
    –   Use pharmacokinetic and pharmacodynamic data for dose, gender, age, ethnic, and environmental effects
    –   Revise carcinogenicity bioassay requirements
    –   Integrate modern biostatistical methods
    –   Use pharmacoepidemiologic data to assess safety and efficacy
    –   Use simple study designs

2. Adopt worldwide dossier/information technology
    –   Harmonise requirements
    –   Electronic vs. paper
    –   Reduce volume of submissions

3. Proactive regulations
    –   Guidelines re gene therapy, pharmacoeconomic data

4. Shared reviews/mutual recognition
    –   CPMP and PER Scheme models

5. Focused dialogue/action
    –   ICH model

6. Integrate checks and balances
    –   QA the regulators
    –   Mutual recognition of GLP, GCP, GMP

IIb and III is increasingly difficult to discern. Given statistically robust results from well-powered, multicentre studies, the classic requirement for replicative pivotal studies should be modified.

Much of the so-called "regulatory creep" is, I suggest, sponsor-generated to atone for imperfect experimental designs at the start. Thus, science could be better served by clarity rather than quantity. Patients are precious, they are in need of prompt therapeutic advice and would be better served by better experiments.

While sponsors are not capable of influencing it, the dynamic of pricing and reimbursement studies must be channelled in a more scientifically productive direction. Almost a second registration exercise becomes necessary in some markets where, more often than not, the economic assessors are less familiar with the principles of clinical research, biostatistics and drug development. If *post hoc*, underpowered, subset analyses cannot be allowed for product claims, they similarly should not be used to limit indications.

Clearly, the issue of harmonisation of the submission document itself has yet to be completely solved. Personal experience on the ICH Efficacy Topic 3 (Clinical Study Reports: Structure and Content) Expert Working Group to develop one clinical study report has highlighted that concessions from each geographic area can be made with science as the driver. As for mutual recognition, or shared reviews, it is just not feasible in the near future to simply mandate the entire dossier to be mutually recognised. On the other hand there are sections (i.e. the preclinical) that are least controversial and may lend themselves to a degree of mutual recognition.

An electronic dossier is my ideal. It may save little in the way of time, but certainly will reduce human error and much of the manpower and material resources required, to say nothing of the trees. A recent abridged application was captured on a single CD (compact disk) rather than needing roughly 100 volumes of text. Internally it saved the company US$1 million in reproduction, paper and delivery costs.

Lastly, the concept of increased quality assessment of the assessors should be supported. Much valuable time is being lost by outlier questions, tangential to quality, safety, and efficacy. No organisation, no matter how excellent, would fail to benefit from checks and balances.

Future challenges

Lest the tasks already outlined be not daunting enough, even greater challenges await. More complex disease processes remain to be solved, and demands for prompt access to safe therapies are ever intensifying. There will be increasing pressure to develop, review and approve agents from novel therapeutic classes, such as DNA-containing and gene-modifying products (Brown *et al.*, 1995). Research and development costs are spiralling (DiMasi *et al.*, 1995; Drews, 1995). Healthcare resource limitations will require data on health economic outcomes, which data will inevitably, in some cases, add to the confusion between therapeutic and economic goals (Canadian Coordinating Office for Health Technology Assessment, 1994). Moreover, the pharmacoeconomic benefits of interventions will require further justification (Clemens *et al.*, 1995). Meanwhile, the patient and taxpayer both are likely to increasingly question the process by which we develop and regulate pharmacological agents.

I believe much of the onus for change rests within industry. To quote Professor Lasagna of the Center for the Study of Drug Development, *"the ultimate NDA's are essentially self-reviewing because all the important questions have been addressed"* (Lasagna, 1995).

Nonetheless, this is not simply a dialogue between "the golden goose" and "the golden rule". All involved must increasingly meet and compromise rather than talk past each other. The ICH initiatives must be sustained and the future beyond ICH3 be clarified. Regardless of all dialogue, regardless of all harmonies and disharmonies, sponsors and regulators alike must not lose sight of their collective mission: the improvement of the public health by rapid introduction and application of medical advances.

References

Brown JS, DiMasi JA, Gosse ME, Manocchia M, Kaitin KI and Shulman SR (1995). Incentives for the development of drugs for AIDS and other life-threatening illnesses: Points to consider. *Bulletin of Tufts Center for the Study of Drug Development*, 1–5.

Canadian Coordinating Office for Health Technology Assessment (1994). *Guidelines for Economic Evaluation of Pharmaceuticals: Canada*, 1st edn. Ottawa, CCOHTA.

Clemens K, Townsend R, Luscombe F, Mauskopf J, Osterhaus J and Bobula J (1995). Methodological and conduct principles for pharmacoeconomic research. *PharmacoEconomics*, 8: 169–174.

DiMasi JA, Hansen RW, Grabowski HG and Lasagna L (1995). Research and development costs for new drugs by therapeutic category. *Pharmaco-Economics*, 7: 152–169.

Drews J (1995). The impact of cost-containment on pharmaceutical research and development. *CMR Annual Lecture.*

Gould AL, Rossouw JE, Santanello NC, Heyse JF and Furberg CD (1995). Cholesterol reduction yields clinical benefit: a new look at old data. *Circulation*, **91**: 2274–2282.

Harris RZ, Benet LZ and Schwartz JB (1995). Gender effect in pharmacokinetics and pharmacodynamics. *Drugs*, **50**: 222–239.

Lasagna L (1995). FDA reform: No more "Business as Usual." *Tufts Center for the Study of Drug Development Newsletter*, **20**: 1.

McAuslane JAN, Lumley CE and Walker SR (eds.) (1992). *The Carcinogenicity Debate*. Lancaster: Quay Publishing.

Peto, R (1990). Meta-analysis in the breech. *Science*, **249**: 476–480.

Simon G, Wagner E and Vonkorff M (1995). Cost-effectiveness comparison using "real world" randomised trials: the case of new anti-depressant drugs. *Journal of Clinical Epidemiology*, **48**: 363–373.

Spielberg SP (1995). Pharmacogenetics: from scientific curiosity to central theme in drug development and therapeutics. *Canadian Journal of Pharmacology*, **2**: 54–56.

Strom BL and Carson JL (1990). Use of automated databases for pharmacoepidemiology research. *Epidemiolical Revues*, **12**: 87–107.

Zeger SL and Liang KY (1986). Longitudinal data analysis for discrete and continuous outcomes. *Biometrics*, **42**: 121–130.

16 What strategies should be considered for implementation by the end of the century? MHW perspective

KAORU MISAWA

Summary

1. New drug development in Japan is as active as in the USA or Europe. However, in comparison with other regulatory agencies, the Ministry of Health and Welfare (MHW) has relatively few staff engaged in new drug review.

2. The review process starts with a provisional internal review including audits of raw data, consultations with industry and GLP and/or GCP inspections, if necessary. This is followed by a comprehensive review by the Central Pharmaceutical Affairs Council (CPAC), an advisory body comprised of external experts, divided into 11 sub-committees.

3. The reality of GCP in Japan makes Japanese clinical trials and drug development unique in the world. The principal investigator has extensive responsibilities, while those of the sponsor are rather limited.

4. A number of improvements to the drug regulatory process in Japan were made during the 1980s. A project team has now been convened by the MHW to recommend ways for continuing improvements. Strengthening manpower and providing a diversity of professions within the Ministry, to help speed the review process, are necessary, as is continued commitment to the International Conference on Harmonisation (ICH) process.

Table 16.1 NCE applications and approvals in Japan

	1990	1991	1992	1993	1994
Clinical trials	155	124	129	160	115
Applications	37	51	67	45	33
Approvals	33	35	31	40	45

Introduction

A number of improvements to the regulatory process for new drug reviews in Japan, were made in the 1980s. Statistics on new drug review in Japan in the 1990s indicate the number of notifications from sponsors of their intention to start clinical trials on a new chemical entity (NCE) for the first time in Japan (Table 16.1). Currently the MHW offers no systematic consultation service on clinical trials for sponsors, except in the case of orphan drug development. Assessors review the submission together with some background information including trial protocols, and may forward questions and/or instructions to the sponsors if appropriate. The numbers of NCE applications and approvals are also shown (Table 16.1). Since the time between application and approval is currently 2 years, the number of approvals may exceed that of applications (as in 1994). These data show that new drug development in Japan is as active as in the USA or Europe and also indicates the efficiency of the MHW.

Comparison of regulatory agencies

A comparison of resources among different regulatory agencies shows that the MHW has a relatively small staff in charge of new drug review (Table 16.2). Within the Ministry, the Pharmaceuticals and Cosmetics Division (PCD), with 38 members, including support staff, is responsible for new drug review. In the Drug Organisation, there are 14 professional staff who are in charge of consultative work for orphan drug development and GLP inspections. The Drug Organisation is a semi-governmental body that was originally established in 1984 to give assistance to patients suffering from adverse

Table 16.2 A comparison of regulatory agencies

	Japan	USA	EC	UK	France
Regulatory agency staff numbers	MHW/PAB 184 PCD 38 Drug Org 14	FDA CDER 741 CBER 643	EMEA 100+	MCA Evaluation 319 244	FMA Evaluation 400 150
Advisory committee size	CPAC 550 New drugs 200	CDER 17 com CBER 4 com 10 experts/com	CPMP 30 Advisory com of 15 MS	CSM 22 4 expert com 60	CAMM 24 External experts 510
Processing time	1 year 6 months	180 days 360 days	300 days	71 working days	120 + 90 days
User fee Local currency $US	JPY 750,000 8,000	US$ 208,000 208,000	ECU 140,000 140,000	GBP 97,500 154,000	FF 100,000 20,000

141

drug reaction (ADR) damage; new duties have since been added, such as assistance to new drug development and orphan development, GLP inspections, and the preliminary review of generic drugs etc.

The Central Pharmaceutical Affairs Council (CPAC) advises the Minister of Health and Welfare on drug policy and registration from the medical, pharmaceutical and scientific points of view. In CPAC, there are 550 experts from universities, hospitals etc. working for the Council on a part-time basis. Of these experts, 200 are engaged in new reviews. The MHW system is more or less similar to that of the French Medicine Agency, particularly in that it depends heavily on external experts for the review of new drugs.

A standard processing period for the assessment of new drugs (currently 18 months) has been established within the Ministry. The actual duration from application to approval is somewhere around 2 years. An examination of these figures indicate that the processing period in MHW compares favourably with other agencies. There is a need to decrease this period, but this may only be possible by strengthening the review staff in the Ministry and CPAC, and by increasing the user fee. Currently, the application fee is moderate at 750,000 Japanese yen, which is equivalent to 8,000 US$ or 5,000 pounds sterling.

New drug review process

In Japan a provisional review of the application for a new drug is made by a team of two or three in-house assessors. Since there are only 13 in-house assessors, one assessor has several pending applications at a time. During the provisional review, several rounds of discussions and consultations are convened, together with audits of raw data, in order to make sure the submitted documents are appropriate for full review by the CPAC. When applicable, GLP inspection (by the Drug Organisation) and/or GCP inspection is conducted.

After completion of the provisional review, the new drug application (NDA) is subject to extensive review by the CPAC, which has 11 sub-committees on different categories of new drugs. The composition of a sub-committee on new drugs is: 1 analytical chemist, 2 toxicologists, 1 pharmacologist, 1 expert on pharmacokinetics, 1 bio-statistician and 7–10 clinicians in fields relevant to the specific category of medicine under review. The sub-committee may meet from two to more than five times, depending mainly on the quality of submitted documents and each meeting may produce some questions to the applicant which have to be answered in writing. Sometimes the committee also gives instructions to conduct additional tests or clinical trials as necessary; these questions and instructions are, of course, open to debate.

Once the review is complete the sub-committee produces an executive summary of the review that is submitted, with necessary documents and data from the applicant, to one of three special committees. The special committee oversees the application from a wider point of view and is, in many cases, authorised to make a final decision according to standard procedures. In the case of innovative drugs or orphan products, the executive committee has to look at the report from the special committee. On the recommendation of the Chairman of the CPAC, the Minister of Health and Welfare will make a decision on the approval of the product.

Internal review

Of the 13 in-house assessors there is only one medical doctor; the others are all pharmacists. In my personal view, the number of assessors must be increased significantly to meet the current need. Also, assessors with different academic backgrounds, such as more medical doctors, pharmacologists, toxicologists, pathologists, and bio-statisticians etc. are required. In addition to the previously outlined activities relating to the provisional review, the in-house assessors act as secretaries to the sub-committees on new drugs, where they are the interface between the applicants and the experts in the sub-committees.

Once or twice a year, staff in the Ministry accumulate their experience from discussions and consultations with industry. A list of questions and answers is produced and industry invited to attend

Table 16.3   Improvement in regulatory process in the 1980s

- Clarifying criteria for foreign clinical data acceptance
- 'Standard Processing Time' for drug registration
- Periodical approval of new drugs and their inclusion in NHI
- Provision of opportunity to hear from CPAC experts

a 1- or 2-day session when the real meaning of those questions and expected answers are explained.

Improvements in the regulatory process

There were improvements made to the drug regulatory process in Japan during the 1980s mainly as a result of the Japan–USA Market Oriented Sector Selective (MOSS) talks, or Japan–EC expert meetings (Table 16.3). The criteria for acceptance of foreign clinical data were clarified. The prevailing belief that MHW accepts no foreign clinical data is not true. Such data are accepted. However, there is still a requirement for some Phase II and Phase III data in Japanese subjects. In the ICH process there have been extensive discussions as to whether the MHW can accept further data that do not include Japanese subjects.

Promoting R&D

The MHW is now as interested in regulating companies as in assisting companies who wish to develop drugs that it thinks are particularly required for the improvement of the public health; in many cases these are not very profitable drugs. Also, the MHW is keen to assist the development of really innovative technologies, even if the chance of success is small. The intellectual properties of drug technologies are therefore protected. The development of orphan drugs is supported with financial assistance, and pre-consultation for clinical and also for registration assistance is provided by staff in the Drug Organisation who have experience in drug review in the MHW. The

the MHW. The MHW co-ordinates joint research by the private, government and academic sectors, in which government money is also invested.

There is also a relatively large amount of investment in, and financing of, the development of innovative drug technologies. The MHW is already offering pre-consultations to companies in these initiatives; this offer is also applicable to foreign companies. Companies are encouraged to investigate the possibility of using these channels, in order to build "good relations" with the regulatory authorities.

GCP in Japan

The reality of GCP in Japan illustrates the difficulties facing the harmonisation programme. GCP inspections started in 1992 and, as of 1995, 65 sponsors and 115 hospitals have been inspected. A small number of sponsors and hospitals were not in compliance with GCP. Japanese GCP is a kind of compromise with medical doctors, based on the (false) belief that companies are bad and doctors are good (Table 16.4). The sponsor's responsibility is rather limited whereas the principal investigator has considerable responsibility for management and for such duties as establishing protocols , collecting and disseminating ADR information, collecting case report forms (CRFs) from investigators, writing study reports, all of which cannot be done without substantial assistance from the company.

There is no explicit provision in Japanese GCP for investigators in a clinical trial to accept monitoring and audit, or regulatory inspection. The investigators report to the principal investigator, not to the sponsor. This is only the tip of the iceberg that makes Japanese clinical trials and drug development unique in the world. The draft ICH GCP document has been translated into Japanese and is being discussed with the medical association. The recent ICH3 discussions in Yokohama provided a good opportunity to expose investigators to the reality of clinical trials in Japan.

145

Table 16.4 Comparison of ICH GCP and Japanese GCP

	ICH GCP	*Japanese GCP*
Sponsor	Protocol QA & QC 　(monitor & audit) Clinical study report	Selection of principal 　investigator Internal audit Information to investigators
Principal investigator	Multi-centre trial only 　(co-ordination)	Management of trial 　Protocol 　ADR information 　Collection of CRF 　Clinical study report
Individual investigators	Conduct of trial Acceptance of 　monitor & audit + 　regulatory inspection Report to sponsor	Conduct of trial Report to principal 　investigator
Informed consent	By document	By document or oral
Internal Review Board	Need external expert	Do not need external expert

Recommendations

The MHW feels partly responsible for this uniqueness. Besides ICH, which has had a substantial impact on the clinical development scene in Japan, the MHW has initiated a project team to find the best way to improve drug development and the regulatory process, in collaboration with associations for the medical professions and pharmaceutical industries. An interim report from this group is expected soon. Possible recommendations include improvement in the quality of clinical development, starting with a comprehensive package of pre-consultation, possibly provided by a semi-governmental body such as the Drug Organisation, with close collaboration with the MHW. Quality Assurance is also one of the important elements. We have to be committed to adopting ICH GCP and to providing timely inspections to prevent non-compliance.

Regarding the review process, the strengthening of manpower is the first priority by not only increasing the number of assessors but also including the different disciplines. The function of provisional review might be outsourced in order for assessors to concentrate on the full review of new drug applications. As yet these are my personal interpretations of the team's discussions.

The future

My personal views for the future are that continued commitment to the ICH process is essential to ensure the efficiency of drug development and the review process. Experiences based on the progress made by ICH should be accumulated and comparable data gathered among the three major regions. With these data, I believe we will be able to make a trilateral comparison of clinical data compatibility. Although it would be very difficult, international joint clinical research, or simultaneous clinical studies with the same clinical protocol, would be very useful to delineate the scientific criteria for the acceptance of foreign clinical data. The quality of data should be supported by quality assurance programmes.

Mutual acceptance of inspection results would provide a good opportunity to create an efficient review process. The possibility of joint training of assessors and inspections should also be sought, to ensure standard evaluation criteria for dossiers and quality of the data. With all this homework done, we would then be able to start thinking about the dreams of global dossiers, mutual recognition and a single agency in the future.

17 What strategies should be considered for implementation by the end of the century? European perspective

ROLF BASS

Summary

1. The new Committee on Proprietary Medicinal Products (CPMP) within the European Medicines Evaluation Agency (EMEA) is striving to develop a European corporate identity. It is comprised of two representatives from each Member State, supported by a network of around 1200 experts.

2. The workload of the CPMP is considerable, as a number of submissions to national authorities made before 1995 have been transferred to the Agency. A tracking system is needed to monitor the progress of applications within the centralised and decentralised procedures.

3. For the future, it will be important to adhere to strict time limits. Sound scientific advice, the enforcement of pharmacovigilance and improved patient information are key issues for the Agency and the CPMP.

Introduction

Although the EMEA only became operational in February 1995, it is timely to discuss the new structures and look into the future. The Agency, and particularly its Permanent Secretariat, is in its infancy; but it has to accommodate all the needs of the industry for a timely review of applications.

A new CPMP

The CPMP has 30 members, two from each Member State, who are appointed by reason of their role and experience in the evaluation of medicinal products. The CPMP ensures appropriate co-ordination between the tasks of the Agency and the national competent authorities, and provides a melting pot of differing expertise from the Member States. Regulatory issues are largely dealt with in a centralised fashion, whereas the scientific part is handled in a more decentralised way.

The new CPMP is very different from the CPMP of the past and it is working hard to develop a European corporate identity. It is supported by a network of approximately 1200 experts from all Member States; many are located within the national competent authorities and others are external experts nominated by those authorities. On the one hand, the selection of experts on behalf of the entire European Union must be transparent, with a list of experts available for interested parties. On the other hand, it may not be advisable to make public the identity of experts as animal rights activists can be very violent. We must find a way to ensure that both agency and external experts remain protected in the future, as they have in the past.

Tasks of the CPMP

The tasks of the CPMP embrace the centralised procedure for European marketing authorisation, arbitration in the decentralised procedure, provision of scientific advice, and co-ordination and assistance to Member States in their pharmacovigilance activities and inspection responsibilities. In addition, submissions made either under the concertation procedure or the multistate procedure before 1995 have been transferred to the EMEA.

Scientific advice

Scientific or technical questions requiring advice may arise at any point during drug development. The problems are how best to select those questions which need forwarding to the CPMP, how to organise the expertise available within the CPMP, and how binding its advice should be.

The whole issue of advice is under discussion within the Secretariat and the CPMP as they are trying to develop a procedure that will benefit both the CPMP members and their experts, as well as the industry. It has been suggested that precise questions with proposed answers should be supplied by the company. Not all would reach the CPMP for the Secretariat could act as a filter, but the Chairman of the CPMP would be kept informed so that he could interfere with the non-forwarding process if necessary. Undoubtedly, the Agency must carefully minute the procedures and the outcomes which finally lead to answers to the questions.

Based on early experience, it is essential that future procedures provide for speedy answers to questions. It will be necessary to levy a fee for these procedures and to provide a system for tracking them.

Workload

Table 17.1 shows the workload status in mid-September 1995 and estimates for subsequent years. Eighteen former concertation applications to national authorities (pre-1995) have been transformed into central marketing applications; three have been forwarded to the Commission for a decision. In addition, 22 new applications have been received in the centralised procedure, two-thirds on a voluntary basis (List B).

The amount of pre-submission dialogue is reflected by the questions to the EMEA, of which 14 concerning scientific issues were

Table 17.1 EMEA workload estimates*

	Pre-1995 (without fees)	1995 (new)	1996	1997
Human medicines				
Scientific advice	—	20	50	70
Central applications	18	22	25	30
Central variations	10	—	80	200
Inspections	8	10	40	70
Decentral applications	74	30	200	300
Arbitrations	—	5	40	60
Veterinary medicines				
Scientific advice	—	2	5	10
Central applications	1	3	8	10
Central variations	2	3	20	40
Maximum residue limits (MRLs)	300	15	20	20
Inspections	—	2	10	12
Decentral applications	19	5	30	50
Arbitrations	—	2	6	10

*Status: September 1995. The above figures will be updated in the course of 1996

handed on to the CPMP. In four of these, answers have been finalised and forwarded to the companies concerned.

There are 74 decentralised applications from the former concertation procedure and 30 new ones. A number of the outstanding multistate applications from pre-1995 are proving difficult to handle although the CPMP is striving to obtain opinions and complete these.

Electronic submissions and tracking systems

With so many applications and different procedures, a tracking system is needed for the benefit of rapporteurs and co-rapporteurs, Member States, the EMEA and companies. This will not be easy to establish, but a prototype should be available for testing from the end of September 1995. Connected to this, but not as an integral part, will be the applicants' submission; it will therefore assist the Agency secretariat to receive electronic submissions.

Future

For the future, it will be very important to adhere to the strict time limits, which are 210 days in the centralised procedure. Sound scientific advice both pre- and post-submission, the enforcement of pharmacovigilance and improved patient information are key issues for the Agency and the CPMP.

18 What strategies should be considered for implementation by the end of the century? CBER vision

KATHRYN ZOON

Summary

1. A number of regulatory reform initiatives are currently in place, or in the process of finalisation, which will significantly improve the regulatory review process for biological products by the Food and Drug Administration.

2. A report reduction policy has increased the flexibility of industry to make changes to its facilities and processes, and has reduced the number of submissions for review. The proposed interpretation of regulation CFR 601.12 should further reduce the workload.

3. The long-term vision is of an efficient, seamless and managed regulatory process. The goals within the Center for Biologics Evaluation and Research (CBER) strategic plan for 2004 include a high quality research programme to enhance the regulatory mission, leveraged resources, and integrated, interactive information systems.

Introduction

In considering strategies for future implementation by the Food and Drug Administration (FDA), this paper addresses current initiatives and long-term planning from the perspective of the Center for Biologics Evaluation and Research (CBER). Some of the issues also apply to the Center for Drug Evaluation and Research (CDER), but CBER does have different approaches due to the heterogeneity of the products within its responsibility. These include whole blood, blood components and derivatives, allergenic extracts, vaccines, mono-clonal antibodies, biotech derived therapeutics and somatic cell and gene therapy.

Reinventing Government

Report reduction

A number of regulatory reform initiatives have emanated from REGO II, the President's "REinventing GOvernment" directive. These deal with eliminating a number of manufacturing and prod-uct amendments, the use and clarification of use of pilot scale facilities, the revision of labelling requirements for biological prod-ucts, and environmental assessment. The first response from CBER was to issue a report reduction policy statement, aimed at increasing the flexibility of industry to change and make improvements to its facilities and processes. This reduces the amount of paperwork that industry has to submit to the FDA and thereby reduces the CBER review burden.

Taking this process one step further, a proposed interpretation of regulation CFR 601.12 (due to be published in early 1996) was drafted to further increase regulatory flexibility, and to also include blood and plasma products, and labelling – areas excluded from the original report reduction activities. A workload analysis (Figure 18.1) shows that report reduction produced a 24% decrease in biologics submissions. Under the proposed regulation the decrease might reach 50%, with a projected 32% decrease for blood and plasma product submissions.

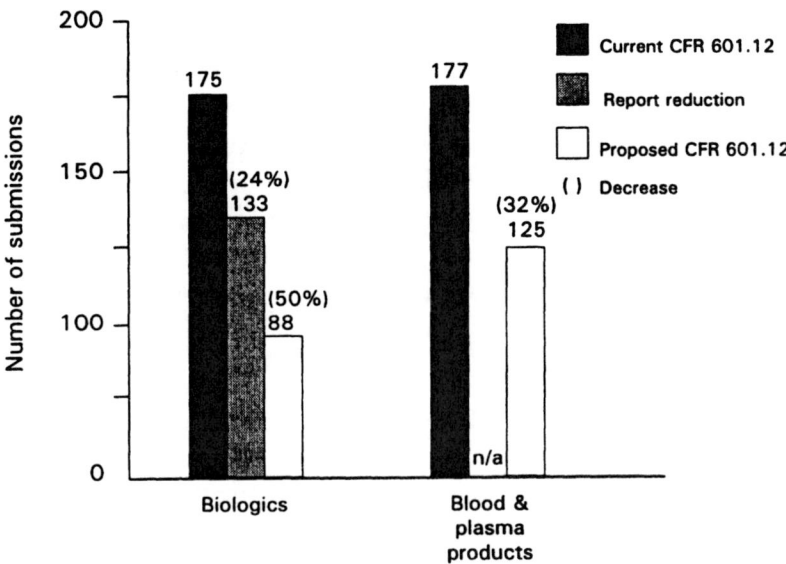

Figure 18.1 Submissions requiring approval prior to implementation

Pilot plants

There has been some confusion and lack of clarity over the licensing requirements for pilot plants; this was of particular concern to small biotechnology companies making large investments in facilities before the results from clinical studies were known. Many manufacturers thought that they needed large-scale facilities in order to obtain product and establishment licences. A new statement issued in June 1995 clarifies the Center's current policy, which is that any facility, pilot or otherwise, may be licensed regardless of scale provided that it meets Good Manufacturing Practices, has an establishment licence application (ELA) and passes its pre-licence inspection. CBER anticipates that companies will now apply for licences for pilot plant facilities. This policy statement also allows for the ELA and the PLA (product licence application) to be submitted at different times to give manufacturers more flexibility. However, the final licences will still be issued simultaneously at the end of the review process.

Labelling

The current requirement in the United States for the manufacturer's name to appear on the licence, the file and the labelling has created some problems, especially with joint ventures. The Center has proposed a rule to allow a distributor's name to appear on the label with the manufacturer's name without regard to precedence or prominence. This should have a big impact on the investment community and companies supporting various drug development procedures.

Environmental impact

Environmental impact studies are extremely costly to the industry and create considerable work for the agencies. In a joint initiative between CBER and CDER it is proposed to allow more drugs to be considered for exclusion from environmental assessment, based upon the minute releases of the drug into the environment as a result of human use.

Other initiatives

Discussions outside the FDA revealed an obvious need for increased flexibility of the licence processes. Consideration is now being given to a number of issues including lot release, standards for biological products, revocation of outdated regulations and elimination of the Establishment Licence for therapeutic recombinant DNA-derived products and monoclonal antibodies.

The FDA is hoping to develop an innovative approach to allow a single application for "well-characterised" product review and approval. To this end, a consensus on the definition of "well-characterised biological product" is required. A Workshop held on 11–13th December 1995 involving the FDA, industry and academia addressed this issue.

Strategic plan

The Center has been working for about a year, on developing a strategic plan for 2004. The first step was to assess and refine the CBER mission, which now reads:

"The mission of the Center for Biologics Evaluation and Research is to *protect* and *enhance* the *public health* through regulation of biological related products including blood, vaccines, and biological therapeutics according to statutory authorities. The regulation of these products is founded on science and law to ensure their purity, potency, safety, efficacy and *availability*."

The key changes shown in italics, reflect a common understanding. The important concepts in the CBER strategic plan have been developed into five major goals as shown in Table 18.1. The vision is of an entire regulatory process that will be efficient, seamless, managed and fully integrated.

A number of strategies have been devised to help achieve these goals. The concepts of managed review will be applied to maximise efficiency and quality assurance; management will be accountable and promote teamwork at all staff levels. Research programmes will underpin the regulatory framework. The application of corporate management principles will promote resource allocation, encourage collaboration and partnerships with other government agencies, industry and academia in research and regulatory processes, and improve information dissemination.

Interactive information systems are integral to all CBER activities. Paperless applications will be the future; INDs, PLAs and NDAs will assume lesser importance once it is possible to create an interactive rolling database for each product. Although this is still far off, assessment of information management systems and electronic submissions is the first step of the way.

International activities

The Center for Biologics Evaluation and Research has played a key leadership role within the International Conference on Harmonisation, since there is a unique opportunity to harmonise guidance in the area of biotechnology. CBER is always willing to work with others on areas of common interest; key international activities are summarised in Table 18.2. These relationships can improve the

Table 18.1 Major goals from CBER strategic plan for 2004

- A managed and integrated regulatory process which is continuous from discovery through post-marketing.

- A high quality research programme which contributes directly to the regulatory mission.

- Leveraged resources and partnerships.

- A high quality diverse work force.

- Interactive information systems, integral to all CBER activities.

Table 18.2 CBER international activities

- International Conference on Harmonisation

- Bilateral activities with Mexico, Canada, and the European Union

- Tripartite activities with the United Kingdom and Canada, Mexico and Canada

- India Project

- Participation with World Health Organization, Children's Vaccine Initiative (CVI), Pan American Health Organization (PAHO), Canada, Mexico, the EU, and the UK

dissemination of information. CBER also works with other countries seeking help with setting up new regulatory systems or who are in need of insight into the management of their processes.

Biologics Manufacturers Assistance Program

The dissemination of information is important. At CBER we have recently instituted a programme to assist biologics manufacturers by making information available by mail, telephone, fax and Internet (Figure 18.2). Additional information and documentation is now available through a page on the World Wide Web which should be helpful not only in the United States but also around the world.

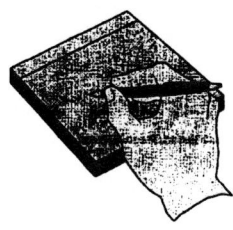

Written Requests:
Division of Congressional and Public Affairs
(HFM-11)
Center for Biologics Evaluation and Research
1401 Rockville Pike, Suite 200N
Rockville, MD 20852-1448, USA

Telephone Information:
Request to speak to staff,
obtain documents, or other info
(301) 594-1800

CBER FAX Information System
available from any FAX with an
attached touchtone phone
(301) 594-1939

Electronic Access:
INTERNET Address:
"CBER_INFO@A1.CBER.FDA.GOV"

WORLD WIDE WEB Address:
"HTTP://WWW.FDA.GOV/CBER/
CBERFTP.HTML"

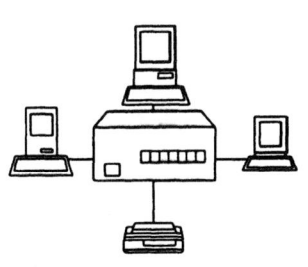

Figure 18.2 CBER Biologics Manufacturers Assistance Program

Conclusion

In conclusion, the Center has already implemented a number of changes in the regulatory process for biologics which have benefited the public, the industry and the agency. There is a need for continued improvement; long-term issues are being addressed through the strategic plan for 2004.

Meeting participants

Mr Michael Arthur
Head of Regulatory &
  Pharmaceutical Affairs
Yamanouchi Pharma Ltd, UK

Professor Sir William Asscher
Principal
St George's Hospital Medical
  School, UK

Professor Rolf Bass*
Head of Human Medicines
  Evaluation Unit
European Medicines Evaluation
  Agency, UK

Dr Susan Bews
Medical Director
Sanofi Winthrop, UK

Dr Paul Branagan
Medical Director/Deputy
  Managing Director
Eisai Europe Ltd, UK

Dr André Broekmans
Executive Director
Medicines Evaluation Board
The Netherlands

Dr George Butler*
Head, International Regulatory
  Group
Zeneca Pharmaceuticals, UK

Mrs Frances Charlesworth
Director, International &
  Commercial Affairs
The Association of the British
  Pharmaceutical Industry, UK

Ms Emer Cooke
Manager, Scientific & Regulatory
  Affairs
European Federation of
Pharmaceutical Industries'
Associations, Belgium

Professor Donald S Davies**
Director, Department of Clinical
  Pharmacology
Royal Postgraduate Medical
  School, UK

Dr Gabrielle Disselhoff
Head, Regulatory Affairs
E Merck, Germany

---

* Syndicate Group Rapporteur
** Syndicate Group Chairman

Ms Emily Donnelly
Director & Senior Vice President
Transnational Regulatory Affairs
 & Compliance
SmithKline Beecham
 Pharmaceuticals, UK

Dr John Donohoe
Head, Drug Toxicology Evaluation
Therapeutic Goods
 Administration, Australia

Dr Hans J Glotz
Head of Regulatory Affairs
Schering AG, Germany

Dr Maria Holz-Slomczyk
Head of Review Department
Bundesinstitut für Arzneimittel
 und Medizinprodukte, Germany

Mr Brenton James
Director, Pharma Regulatory Policy
Glaxo Wellcome Research &
 Development, UK

Dr David Jefferys**
Director, Licensing Division
Medicines Control Agency, UK

Dr Gorm Jensen
Chief Physician, Department of
 Cardiology
Hvidovre Hospital, Denmark

Professor Trevor M Jones
Director General
The Association of the British
 Pharmaceutical Industry, UK

Mrs Sarah Jones
Senior Consultant, Regulatory
 Affairs
Allergan Ltd, UK

Dr Yves Juillet **
Director Pharma Policy
Roussel Uclaf, France

Dr Jacinta Keogh-Bennett
Head of Regulatory Affairs
Ciba, UK

Mr Michael J Krieg
Assistant Vice President
International Regulatory Affairs
Wyeth-Ayerst, USA

Dr John Lechleiter
Vice President, Regulatory Affairs
Lilly Research Laboratories, USA

Dr Cyndy Lumley
Associate Director
Centre for Medicines Research, UK

Mr Bryan W Marlow
Vice President, Regulatory Affairs
 Europe
Solvay, Germany

Ms Vaila M Marshall*
Director, Regulatory Affairs
 Department
Pfizer Central Research, UK

Dr Neil McAuslane
Research Manager
Centre for Medicines Research, UK

Dr Till Medinger
Senior Vice President, Corporate
  Strategy
Zeneca Group, UK

Mr Dann M Michols
Director General of the Drugs
  Directorate
Health Canada, Canada

Mr Kaoru Misawa
ICH Co-ordinator, Pharma &
  Cosmetics Division
Ministry of Health & Welfare
Japan

Dr A P Morgenstern
Director, Corporate Regulatory
  Affairs
Yamanouchi Europe BC
The Netherlands

Dr Alastair Morris
Senior Director, International
  Regulatory Affairs
Johnson & Johnson, Switzerland

Mrs Brenda Mullinger
Medical Writer, UK

Dr Christopher Parkinson
Senior Research Associate
Centre for Medicines Research, UK

Dr Michael S Perry
Vice President, Drug Regulations
  & Regulatory Affairs
Sandoz Pharmaceuticals
  Corporation, USA

Dr Peter Read
Chairman
Hoechst Marion Roussel UK

Mr Fernand Sauer
Executive Director
European Medicines Evaluation
  Agency, UK

Dr David R Savello
Vice President, North American
  Regulatory Affairs
Glaxo Wellcome, USA

Professor Jens S Schou
Chairman, Danish Committee on
  Adverse Drug Reactions
Institute of Pharmacology
Denmark

Ms Viviane Schuermans
Vice President, International
  Registrations
Janssen Research Foundation
Belgium

Dr Eve E Slater
Senior Vice President, Clinical &
  Regulatory Development
Merck Research Laboratories, USA

Mr Ralph Smalling
Director of Regulatory Affairs
Amgen, USA

Dr Christian Spilles
Head of Regulatory Affairs
  International
Bayer, Germany

Professor Kjell Strandberg
Director General
Medical Products Agency, Sweden

Dr Robert Temple*
Director, Office of Drug Evaluation I
Food and Drug Administration
USA

Mr Gerald Thompson
Director of International
  Regulatory Affairs
Synthelabo, France

Professor Stuart Walker
Director
Centre for Medicines Research, UK

Dr Roger Williams
Associate Director for Science &
  Medical Affairs
Center for Drug Evaluation &
  Research
Food and Drug Administration
USA

Dr Dan Zabrowski
Vice President, Drug Regulatory
  Affairs
Hoffmann-La Roche, USA

Dr Manuel Zahn
Head of Regulatory Affairs
Knoll AG, Germany

Dr Robert L Zerbe **
Senior Vice President, Worldwide
  Clinical Research
Parke-Davis Pharmaceutical
  Research Institute, USA

Dr Kathryn Zoon
Director, Center for Biologics
  Evaluation and Research
Food and Drug Administration
USA

Index

CPSIA information can be obtained
at www.ICGtesting.com
Printed in the USA
LVOW10*1226040318

568593LV00009B/912/P

9 780792 387060